pocketbooks

Frontispiece: Sgurr Alasdair and Sgurr Sumain, The Cuillin.

The Way to Cold Mountain

a Scottish mountains anthology

The Way to Cold Mountain

Edited by Alec Finlay
with photographs by David Paterson

pocketbooks
Morning Star Publications
Polygon
An Tuireann

2001

Published by:
pocketbooks
Canongate Venture (5), New Street, Edinburgh, EH8 8BH.

Morning Star Publications
Canongate Venture (5), New Street, Edinburgh, EH8 8BH.

Polygon
22 George Square, Edinburgh, EH8 9LF.

An Tuireann
Struan Road, Portree, Isle of Skye, IV51 GEG.

Typeset in Minion and Univers.
Typesetting and artworking by Bluelines New Media Solutions.
Design concept by Lucy Richards with Alec Finlay.
Printed and bound by Bath Press Limited, Bath.

Published with the assistance of grants from the Scottish Arts Council National
Lottery Fund, the Highlands and Islands Enterprise (HI Arts),

A CIP record is available from the British Library.

ISBN 0 7486 6288 X

List of Contents

Mountain Top

Oh, the conceit of people who succeed in climbing to the top of a mountain! It is the one moment when the obscure may feel that they are standing on a pedestal.

Ramon Gomez de la Serna
translated by Helen Granville-Barker

Editor's Acknowledgements

Nature and landscape have been the most persistent themes to emerge in the pocketbooks series; from the walking practice of Hamish Fulton and Thomas A. Clark, to the haiku in *Atoms of Delight*; proposals in *Without Day*; and the coast and sea in *Green Waters*, Ian Stephen's *Mackerel & Creamola* and Helen Douglas' *Unravelling the Ripple* (Autumn 2001). The common approach that emerges from these different projects is both celebratory and cautionary: the poetics and politics of what remains the defining characteristic of this country.

I would like to thank all of the contributors to this present anthology, in particular David Craig, whose writings on climbing and the history of the Scottish landscape, were one inspiration for the concept of this anthology. Thanks to G. F. Dutton – whose expertise in the subject and dedication to the task produced an extensive survey of mountaineering publications – and the editors of all the journals he has quoted from. I would also like to thank David Paterson, who allowed us to present a selection of the photographs of the mountains and glens of Scotland he has made over the past three decades. Readers can enjoy a wider selection of his photographs in *A Long Walk on the Isle of Skye* (Peak Publishing, 1999).

An exhibition featuring David Paterson's photographs, and a new installation by artist Dan Shipsides, will take place at An Tuireann (Portreee, Isle of Skye), Summer 2001. I would like to thank An Tuireann for their support as copublishers. I would also like to thank Ken Cockburn, Sophy Dale, Alison Humphry, Laura Coxson and Cluny Sheeler at pocketbooks; Simon Williams at Bluelines New Media Solutions; Lucy Richards; Alison Bowden and Emma Darling at Polygon; Thomas A. Clark, Gerry Loose and Colin Will; and also Meg Bateman, Franziska Furter and Anna Kenny.

Alec Finlay

The Joy of Living

Before me is a drawing of Sgurr nan Gillean by a young Swiss artist, Franziska Furter, who was my companion on a visit to Skye last Spring. Many readers will know that dark buttress of rock standing by Sligachan, and the more intrepid will be familiar with the panoramic view of the Quirang, Raasay and Applecross that its summit offers.

It was a strange thing to take a Swiss to the mountains. We set off from Edinburgh one May morning, and spent the first few days resting at Meg Bateman's cottage in Tarskavaig, on the Sleat peninsula. There we had our first view of the Cuillin, drawn like a grey curtain over the bay. Then we took the winding road through Skye to Uig and our CalMac ferry to the Hebrides.

My grandmother, Caitriona, who grew up in Duntuilm in the north-west of Skye, once told me how she hiked those roads in the middle of the war. She was back on leave and walked home from Portree in a blizzard, with the snow reaching above her knees. She was hardy. Her great life-philosophy was the brisk walk taken in the open air, which she held to be a cure-all for introspection and all forms of melancholy. She was forever sending us off up this or that hill. Her father, Seton Gordon, the naturalist and photographer, was a Highland gentleman in the grand old style. An extract from his writings on the Cairngorms is included here, amongst David Craig's selections.

On Berneray, each morning was clearer than the last. Franziska, and I laughed at the new snowfalls on the peaks glinting over the Minch. It was too much to resist, so, on our return journey we hopped-off the bus at Sligachan, signed the hotel register, downed rucksacks, filled the water-bottle from the sink, and set off into the Spring sunshine and along the path that led to the Sgurr. I was fresh from re-reading *Electric Brae*, and, as Andy Greig might have put it, we had the kind of things to talk about that the hills would put on a surer footing.

Franziska wasn't disappointed by Scotland's mountains when she compared them with the Swiss Alps: as she explained, our mountains "rise straight from the sea". Looking at her drawing today, I can pick out the plateau where we let go our ambition, caught our breath, and took in the last of the day. We only got as far as the beginning, but it was somewhere new for me.

For many years illness kept me off the hills, and made them a brooding presence. The first time I went north, to stay with friends in Sutherland, I remember the drive past Suilven, Stac Pollaidh and Cuil Beg, and how they were so eerie, backlit by a dirty purple Atlantic storm. Their beauty was beyond doubt, but the scene that unfolded also held a kind of terror, as if there were only a fragile carapace protecting me from that deathly extent of moor and mountain.

That was a dozen years ago. Last Spring, as I sat and puffed, I knew that the illness was gone, and I gulped in great lungfulls of the joy of living. A few months later I met a beautiful young woman who grew up on Rasaay. Anna's school bus took the road that passes the Cuillin each morning. Something of the island and its mountain views shines in her eyes. Hebridean Romantic just isn't in it. Some things stay with you: Neil Young, singing 'Sugar Mountain', and you're leaving here too soon.

When I make my next journey to the Cuillin I know that the mountains won't have a care amongst them what memories I bring. Nevertheless, memories of journeys, friends and loved-ones, hover around the pages of this book. In David Paterson's photographs a familiar silhouette, crop of rock, or effect of the light, is further evidence of how ingrained this landscape is in my imagination. Readers will bring their own associations to the words and images that are collected here.

* * *

The writers and artists who contributed to *The Way to Cold Mountain* were invited to write an essay suggesting the meaning that the mountains of Scotland holds for them. Some were also invited to add a selection of writings by other authors, not necessarily by Scots, and not necessarily describing Scottish mountains. Along with examples of British mountaineering literature, their selections include masterpieces of prose by Primo Levi, Antoine Saint-Exupery and poetry by Han Shan. The resulting mosaic reveals the different meanings that the wilderness holds; the ways in which cultural meanings have been refined by changing social attitudes; and the development of new literary styles and forms, with which to describe these extremes of physical and mental experience.

Mountains are implacable realities and powerful motifs. From Ben Lawers to Hozomeen or Mount Analogue, they are our most enduring image of completeness. It will come as no surprise that many of the contributions to this anthology echo the Romantic tradition, portraying the individual *in extremis*. Less widely noted by critics of this literature is the underlying sense of community concealed within much writing about mountains. There is perhaps a nostalgia at work here, deriving from an archetypal memory of a mountain-dwelling people. This mythic, native society can be glimpsed in Tacitus and Ossian, or more recently in the work of Hugh MacDiarmid and Kenneth White. White's writings on geopoetics, though couched in terms of scientific precision, are permeated by this nostalgia for *Scotia deserta*, close neighbour to MacDiarmid's rugged stone land.

The climbing fraternity can be seen as a latterday reflection of this community – a clannish brotherhood, adapted to the austerities of the wilderness and bonded by a sense of mutual-aid and courage in adversity. Climbing is the return to an environment that we now find alien and inhospitable. In this light, the writings collected here are so many vision-quests, defining an essentially mythic relationship to the natural landscape, which itself figures as the raw material of the human psyche.

Many of the extracts included here portray physical journeys and the work of artistic creativity as endeavours that go hand-in-hand. The ascent of a mountain gifts the writer a moment of joyful recognition, such as the Austrian novelist, Peter Handke, describes in his homage to Cezanne, *The View from Mont Sainte-Victoire*:

> Yes, this twilit path now belonged to me and became nameable. In addition to innocently uniting the fragments of my own life ... the moment of fantasy (in which I alone am real to myself and know the truth) revealed to me anew kinship with other, unknown lives ... acting as an unspecified love and striving to communicate itself in a form conducive to fidelity, namely, as a justified project aimed at the cohesion of my never-to-be defined nation as our common form of existence.

Even in our technological and nuclear age, when mountains are no longer representative of *the* towering certainty, any of us can turn our back on society and head for a day in the hills, where we will encounter an experience against which we can measure and renew our daily lives. And yet, however meaningful they may be, these experiences remain fleeting, as, at the end of each adventure the writer-climber must inevitably return to the contingencies of the world.

An anthology such as this is denied the overarching symbolic completeness which its theme might, at first, seem to offer. The contemporary writer's inability to express a commonly held sense of ultimate reality, a faith, that would give meaning to these personal spiritual quests, is a direct consequence of the decline in religious belief.

Writing about nature tends to fall into one or other of a host of specialisms – the walker or mountaineer, the botanist or geologist, the painter or poet – each approaching the mountain from a different point of view and appraising us of their particular form of knowedge, whether scientific or imaginative. As Colin Will's essay suggests, these conflicting specialisms represent powerful historical economic and political interests; so many fences and 'No Trespassing' signs, blocking off the paths worn by tinkler, drover, rambler and climber.

Meg Bateman's poem, 'Elgol: Two Views' illustrates the personal nature of our experience of the wilderness perfectly:

Elgol: Two Views

I looked at the old post-card,
the houses like a growth from the soil,
the peaks towering above them,
a sign of the majesty of God,
before an amenity was made of mountains,
or a divide between work and play,
between the sacred and the secular . . .
and I passed the picture to the old man.

"Does it make you sad, Lachie?" I asked
as he scrutined it in silence.
"Sad? Bah! Not at all!
I couldn't place her for a moment,"
and he pointed to a cow in the foreground.
"That's the Yellow Lady, the Red Lady's second calf –
I'd know any cow, you see,
that belonged here in my lifetime."

David Craig has discussed the differences between contemporary and former attitudes to climbing, as revealed in mountain literature, in his survey *Native Stones*. In many ways this anthology bears out his arguments, only differing in its shift of emphasis away from the English Romantic poets and onto Scottish writers, such as MacDiarmid and White who represent later forms of Romanticism. These authors share a Nietzschean vision of the wilderness, and although the tone is softer, White's writing is often reminiscent of MacDiarmid's identification with a supra-mortal mental force, released through mountain experiences. A change of attitudes is evident if we compare this sense of 'austere intoxication' with the feelings of frailty that Gerrie Fellows and Tom Prentice describe when faced with the uncontrollable forces of nature. Once safely home, socks drying by a warm fire, they admit that in writing they can only catch hold of 'a fragment . . . a moment of knowledge'.

The work of the young artist contributors to this anthology brings us up to date. Dan Shipsides reflects the new mountain writing, drawing on the Extreme-style of American West Coast zines. Climbing is central to Shipsides' art practice. In recent installations he has been scaling gallery walls, recreating famous climb-routes, and leaving scrapes and dents on the walls, and a real-time video, as evidence.

The piece featured here, 'Beta', describes the repeated physical movements which are the essence of any climb, a performance which could take place 3,000 feet above a sheer drop, or on an indoor climbing wall. The transcription of these restricted gestures is a reminder of one of the paradoxes of climbing: placed amongst beautiful scenery, the climber's view is often limited to a few feet of rockface.

No spiritual verities hover around the Extreme-climber, just an adrenalin high and the urge to push on. Neal Beggs' recent public art commission (for CCA Glasgow), extracts of which are included here, catalogues in mundane fashion the herculean task of climbing all of Scotland's Munros and Glasgow's Tower Blocks. The artist ticks them off, one-by-one: bare facts that stand for themselves alone.

Another contemporary artist whose work shares this new mood is Ross Sinclair. In his well-known installation 'Real Life Rocky Mountain' (1996), Sinclair sits with his back to us, on a mound of fake astro-turf wilderness, surrounded by stuffed animals and kitsch detritus. His marathon performance is to sing Scottish songs from the last two hundred years: like Beggs, he reduces a Romantic trial to a chore. Sinclair combines Jacobite nostalgia with post-punk angst, pitching Scotland's youth – alienated from the land, alienated from the literary traditions of the land – against a familiar misty Highland setting. 'Lost' is where we are.

Another recent work, Angus Farquhar's performance 'The Path', which took place in Glen Lyon, was concerned with spiritual experience and pilgrimage. The atmosphere of this event depended on bringing Tibetan performers into the Scottish landscape. The need to import examples of 'world culture' to give veracity to the spiritual experience of landscape supports the idea that there is a crisis in our ability to represent that experience in terms of our own culture.

This anthology concludes in ultra-contemporary style with an alphabetic sampler from a current climbing website. From this contemporary vantage point, where love for tradition and post-punk nihilism jostle, we look back to the diminishing figures of Wordsworth, Ruskin and W. H. Murray further down the glen.

* * *

There are still mountain anthologies being published which represent the transcendentalist Wordsworthian tradition of the Romantic wanderer. *The Way to Cold Mountain* is not one of them. Its concern is to present a brief survey of the subject, its spiritual, cultural and political meanings, and to investigate the different ways in which authors have approached writing about the Scottish mountains over the past two hundred years. Its politics are those of the Rambler and Bothy parties; however, its essential position is that the mountains are *gestalt* and that they represent a touchstone for how we relate to the land.

There is enough climbing lore here to entertain someone holed up in a bivvy for the duration of a blizzard. This anthology is not only intended for adepts of the climbing cult: it is for anyone who loves these withheld places. Put a copy in your pocket; read it sitting in a car with a thermos of coffee on the dashboard; resting beneath an azure sky on a grassy plateau; or balanced on the summit trig point.

Alec Finlay

Dedicated to the memory of my grandmother, Caitriona Macdonald Lockhart; and to Meg Bateman, Franziska Furter and Anna Kenny.

Cold Mountain

Men ask the way to Cold Mountain.
Cold Mountain: there's no through trail.
In summer ice doesn't melt
The rising sun blurs in swirling fog.
How did I make it?
My heart's not the same as yours.
If your heart was like mine
You'd get it and be right here.

Han-shan
translated by Gary Snyder

Mountain Walking

Kenneth White

Mountain Walking
Mountain contemplations imprinted on the mind. ('Scotia deserta')

Since I'm writing from France, or rather from the Armorican peninsula, which was a high mountain (for long the only emergent part of what was to be France) before it got ground down into a rugged fragmented peneplain by forces such as the Atlantic Ocean, let me begin by quoting a couple of French texts on the Scottish mountains. In one, an essay in the *Revue générale des sciences pures et appliquées* (Paris, 1892) later published as a threepenny booklet, Marcel Bertrand says this: 'The Caledonian chain is one of the oldest, if not *the* oldest, that we can reconstitute. We're confronted there by movements of the earth's crust that go back to the beginning of primary times.' And he concludes by saying that anyone interested in metamorphism (who with any sense *can't* be interested in metamorphism?) should make a pilgrimage to the coasts of Scotland. In the other text, this time a weighty volume of about seven hundred pages, the result of long years of tectonic, lithological and petrographic investigations, the most thorough study of geomorphology in Scotland I know of, *Recherches de géomorphologie en Écosse du Nord-Ouest* (Strasburg, 1965), Alain Godard says that before actually going up there he'd never realised just how rich in morphostructural combinations the bedrock of Scotland was.

About five hundred million years ago (for the oldest rocks, you'd have to go back something like three thousand million, but let's be reasonable), Scotland stood at the edge of a continent that linked up Scandinavia, Greenland and North America. About four hundred and fifty million years ago, the country was south of the Equator, separated from England (ah, blessed times!) by a great stretch of tumultuous water. It was only about sixty million years ago that, with the widening of the Atlantic (it's still widening, while the Pacific is getting narrower), Scotland lost its contact with the large lands of the North-West and got stuck with England, for Britain or for worse.

As a kid on the west coast of Scotland, I had the island of Arran, which is an epitome of Scotland as a whole, in front of me day after day, and in particular the lines of Goatfell. This was in Ayrshire (latitude 55° to 56° North, longitude 4° to 5° West), to some extent cut off from the rest of the country ('Out of the world and into the Lairgs' was an old phrase) by the Kilbirnie Hills and the Fenwick moors. It was on these hills and moors that I did my first mountain walking, between, say, the Craigie Rock at the north end of Fairlie and the Kaim, which looms gloweringly over the whole area.

Arran came later. I'd start out from Brodick where, unless of course it's raining (which happens now and then), you see Goatfell rising in pale-blue lines, and Glen Rosa maybe bathed in a strange light. If, by the way, anybody thinks Glen Rosa has anything to do with rosiness, he or she should think again: it's from old Norse *hross-a* (the river of the horse). From Brodick (right, the 'broad bay'), I'd cross the island to Blackwaterfoot on Kilbrannan (St Brandan's) Sound, then make along the coast, in the company of sleek seals and blue-beaked fulmars, by Whitefarland (*huitt-for-landi*, 'the white land between the sea and the hills'), Catacol ('the valley of the wild cats') up to Lochranza. Beyond Lochranza lie the strata of schist and sandstone on which, after a good close read at them, James Hutton was to base his theory of non-conformity, which was proof that the earth *moved*, that it had been subject to change, and still was. With Hutton, the mind moved from any notion of a static world to a world that was fluctuant, dynamic, geostrophic. It was with all this in my head (accumulation of matter, forces of erosion and transformation, ideas of composition) that I'd walk along the slopes of Goatfell, Beinn Tarsuinn or Beinn Nuib.

I say 'walk along'. I've never had any truck with the notion of 'conquering' mountains, and I loathe mountaineering considered as a sport. I'm not concerned with exploits, technical performances, drama or adventure. What I'm interested in, involved in, is an understanding of the mountain and the experience of the mountain, a *high* experience of the mountain, founded on the encounter with brute matter, and with wind, light, space, emptiness.

In the outlying islands of Scotland, the brute matter will be Lewisian gneiss. On the north-west coast, the original gneiss will be overlaid by a thick layer of red sandstone, the residue of ancient hyperborean river-systems, with the gneiss sometimes breaking through, eroded into all kinds of twisted, tworled shapes. Further inland, it will be igneous again on the top – rock such as schist, quartz and granite. The wind and the light also come in many forms, many forces, many sheens and shades. As for space and emptiness, they are harder to seize, harder for our all too agitated minds to get into.

I've spent hours and days walking over these rocks. Even when I felt the need, existentially and intellectually, to break away from a British socio-cultural context of which Scotland was, willy-nilly, a part, I kept coming back to them. I could curse a phoney political set-up, I could curse a murky social context, I could curse all the thick shit-lit that was piling up on the pavements, I couldn't curse the depths and heights, the darknesses and lights of Drumalban, that line of mountains going from the waters of the Clyde right up to Cape Wrath, which Adam Bede in his *Historia* (eighth century) calls *dorsum Brittaniae*, 'the backbone of Britain' and which Fordun, in his *Scotichronicon* (fifteenth century) evokes as 'those great mountains that cross the middle of the country, like the high Alps of Europe'.

As a Scot in Europe (over the centuries, so many Scoto-Celtic minds have had to make back there for breathing space and mental scope), I kept frequenting mountains. They extended my landscape and mindscape, while keeping me in touch with what was highest (and most vigorous – I'm not talking about any solemn loftiness, any snobbish snootiness, any highfalutinness) in my native background.

At one time, I did a lot of walking in the Austrian Alps, around the Ötztal. Just a few miles away lay the plateau of the Engadine where, in the late nineteenth century, Friedrich Nietzsche spent the most inspired part of his life, describing himself as '6,000 feet above humanity and the age'. Again (in a high shared culture, this kind of explaining wouldn't be necessary) let no one read into that phrase an expression of inhuman contempt. See in it rather the criticism and refusal of certain conceptions and habits of 'Humanity' (with a capital H) that prevent the human being from being what he or she *can* be. As for the age, nobody in his right mind, with any sense of comparative culture, could claim that the age Nietzsche lived in, and that we're still living in, was the best that civilisation has ever known. Which doesn't prevent anyone working at potentiality (in secluded, mountainous areas, for example), and maybe writing a good book or two, which, in the long run, is the best thing you can do for other people anyway.

It was with perspectives like these that I lived for sixteen years in the Pyrenees.

In one of his notebooks written at Black Mountain, in North Carolina, Charles Olson writes, longingly, of 'a fresh experience of place: those caves, the Pyrenees, old France, old Spain, old earth, just fresh out ice, etc., those animals'. That, along maybe with a few other things, is what I was into during those Pyrenean years.

At the beginning of the second volume of his *Universal Geography*, Elisée Reclus (a great friend, by the way, of Patrick Geddes), who was brought up in these parts, says of the Pyrenean region that, from the points of view of anthropology and sociology, but especially of geology, it constitutes 'a world apart'. The first intimate comment on that 'world apart' came to me from a little blue booklet I picked up in a secondhand bookshop in Pau. This was by an Irishman, Henry Russell-Killough, who had been all over the world, from Siberia to Calcutta (another of his books is entitled *Memories of a Mountaineer*), before settling down there in South-West France. Russell made a living toting British tourists about, but he loved the Pyrenees, calling them wild, immaculate and, compared to the Alps, 'female'. He ended up finding himself a grotto on the Vignemale, at about 10,000 feet, which he transformed into a hermitage he called Le Paradis, where he'd drink champagne in the company of the last bears.

I've been in all the Pyrenean valleys and walked along their slopes, but the one I frequented most was the Ossau, the 'valley of the bears' – maybe the territory of some paleolithic community, the Bear Clan. I'd go up by Bielle, then by Laruns and Artouste, and continue in winter on snowshoes. There was a little place up there I frequented a lot, the Col de Marie-Blanque. You might think Marie Blanque refers to a woman. In fact it refers to a bird, the *mari-blanque* in Bearnese, *behibedeko emazte xuria* in Basque: *neophron perancopterus*. The Pyrenean region is still one of the best places in Europe for observing such birds. I remember up on the plateau of Urculu watching a band of twenty vultures, and they watching me. In addition to mari-blanques, vultures, eagles, falcons and hawks, you'll see the bird Spaniards call 'the bone-breaker', *quebranta huesos*. Just across the Spanish border was Monte Perdido – and what a delight was that, walking along the canyon path, say in the early morning redness of an Autumn day and the grey, snow-streaked mass of the Perdido rising just above you.

When I came to write the *Pyrenean Meditations*, I had in mind a Pali phrase, 'he contemplates the thought of light', and I tended to equate the Pyrenees with *prajñaparamita*, the perfection of wisdom.

With mountains, how crazy can you get?

The West-East thing was in fact something I'd been working at over the years, and it all just intensified, while also spacing itself out, there in the Pyrenees. 'If only I could make tracks to the original desire that lives back of reason!' cries Manuel de Diéguez in *The Rationalist Myth of the West* and, later on: 'If only I could inhabit deep emptiness.' That's exactly what I was doing around the Pic du Midi d'Ossau, the Vignemale and Monte Perdido. In the studio ('The Residence of Solitude and Light') in Pau, as well as pretty tough texts on logic and epistemology, I was reading a lot of Chinese mountain-poetry. Here's Wang Wei for example: 'These beautiful days in Hsiang-Yang make drunken my old mountain heart.' Here's Dogen: 'The real mind, what is it? I can't say. Just look at the snow on the mountains.' And I liked what Fan K'uan had said of himself – that he had walked over a thousand miles in order to get to know 'the bones of the mountains'.

It was logical (geo-logical) that I should continue my mountain-lines in the East. As the result of circumstances and chance (but maybe there's a deep underlying poetic logic), that took place in Northern Japan, in the Three Mountain Region, and on Hokkaido (the 'North Sea Road').

The 'Three Mountains' are Haguro, Gassan and Yudono. They used to be frequented a lot, and still are to some extent, by the Shinto-buddhist *yamabushi*, for whom the most sacred of texts is the natural context. In the Nô play, *Kagyu*, it's a *yamabushi* who comes first on stage, saying: 'I'm from Mt Haguro, and I've just been to Mt Omine and Mt Kazuraki. Walking in the mountains, sleeping on the moors, the life of the *yamabushi* is an ascetic exercise.' What the *yamabushi* is ultimately out for is supernatural power (*ken*). This Ken was just out for mountain poetics (high, open poetics). Here, as I walked in the clear air, it was haiku after haiku:

All alone
With an old crow
In unfamiliar country

In the mountains
On the banks of a torrent
Drinking cold sake

When I pushed on later up to the Hokkaido, across the Straits of Tsugaru, I made for Daisetsuzan, 'big snow mountain'. What I went into there was a long snowy meditation that put enough coolness into my mind to last me for a year or two at least.

But in a complete poetic economy, not only coolness is required, but also fieriness – just as any transcendentalism needs a descendentalism to give it grit and pith.

The last time I did a fiery walk was just a few months back, on the island of Reunion, in the Indian Ocean, where vulcanism is still active. If Reunion's original volcano, the Piton des Neiges (Snow Peak) is now quiet, La Fournaise (The Furnace) still pours out bright lava every now and then.

First of all, you cross the Plain of Sands, a dark red desert of old volcanic dust, by a narrow track that takes you to the rim of the live crater. What vegetation there is on the rim is that of a stunted moorland: lichens, silvery-stemmed shrubs ... You then enter the Enclosure. It's a weathered paleo-lava field with old craters rising here and there: grey piles with gaping red maws. After a while the path gets steeper and you're scrambling over lava rock till you come to the edge of the Bory. You then move east along the Bory till you come to the Dolomieu: a cauldron with smoke rising here and there. When it got too hot, I moved away and found myself a cool place to rest with my back against a rock: down in the Enclosure, an absolute landscape, a landscape pushed to the limit of abstraction, with no less than thirty absolutely perfect little fujiyamas.

During that walk, I picked up a dozen pieces of lava, some opaque and contorted, brown, orange or red, others porous, black with blue and green iridescences, and was carrying them in my rucksack. They're now set out on a table in my workroom, beside Johnson's *Physical Atlas of Natural Phenomena* (Edinburgh, 1850) opened at 'Mountain Chains in Asia and Europe' that brings out in a strong graphic design the mountains-lines from Scotland to Japan.

There's a logic in it all, and more than a logic.

It's this kind of thing I keep trying to work out.

World-lines.

Emergent fields.

Kenneth White

Reading Han Shan in the Pyrenees

1.

The disciples of Buddha
called him 'poet-monk'
those of Lao-Tzu called him
'hermit and mystic'
and the Confucianists said he was
a crazy eccentric
who sometimes talked sense

for himself
he was just Cold Mountain
doing his best
never knowing exactly
where it was leading him.

2.

Du Guangting (850-933)
in his Shanxian Shiyi
says Han Shan
'lived on Mt Cuiping
in the Tiantai Mts'

for the Taoists
the Tiantai range
was one of those places
'where men grow wings'

every now and then
he'd go down to the Guoqing monastery
to get food from the kitchen
but mostly he was up there
among the white clouds.

3.

    Hadn't always been there though
    talks of Red Sparrow Street
    in Chang'an
    where he must have raised the dust
    (memories of sweet little girls:
   'young girls playing in the twilight
    the breeze blows their perfume over the road')
    before making for the heights.

4.

    An unorthodox character
    outside the classifications
    he'd do a little zazen when it suited him
    but made fun of the 'straight backs'
    and 'shaven pates' in general

    tao-buddhist, okay
    but let's just say
    mountain-poet
    and get into the poems

    all three hundred and eleven of them.

5.

   'A certain smart alec by the name of Wang
    said my poems were all wrong
    and that I had no sense of prosody
    they make me laugh with their "correct" poetry
    it's just blind men singing about the sun'
    let me find one man with clear eyes
    said Han Shan
    and my poems will go round the world.

6.

  'I sauntered off to see a great monk
  misty mountain, mile after mile
  the old fellow showed me the way back home:
  the round lamp of the moon'

  'strolling about on Huading Mt
  sky clear, marvellous day'

  'when the moon's bright
  and all white
  you can forget about East and West'.

7.

  These Cold Mountain poems
  are like a day with two dawns.

Kenneth White

41

First and Last Climbs
David Craig

First and Last Climbs

On 7 October 1952, my twentieth birthday, I climbed rock for the first time – with a rope, that is – on the Black Spout Pinnacle of Lochnagar. As I stood staring up at the dark, impending mass of it, which looked impossibly steep and no place for humans, a voice called out of the sky, "Hiya, Davie! Fancy seeing you here!", or words to that effect. And there was Bill Brooker, at ease on the rockface, his feet on nothing very much, a rope spiralling from his waist to an invisible belayer somewhere round the corner. Thirty years later I found out that his companions had been Tom Patey and Mike Taylor and they were putting up a new route called The Stack.

Bill was then a chief pioneer of the post-War wave in rock and ice climbing. I had been at school with him in Aberdeen from 1937 to 1950, at the university since then, although our ways had diverged in our teens. In the later 1980s, as we both approached retirement, I rang him from three hundred miles away in Cumbria and we renewed our friendship. In no time we were enjoying the first stages of climbing together into our old age.

Bare rock had not been my experience of the Cairngorms. I walked through them, round them, up them, feeling those rounded masses pressing in, slowly clenching on you, as a grain of corn might feel the embrace of the millstones. To reach the next unfolding of a glen, and then the next, became the most satisfying sort of journeying in the world, with that straightening-up at the end of it as you sloughed off your ex-Commando rucksack and got ready to make cakes out of powdered potato and griddle them on top of a stove stuffed with pine logs. The slow rising and massing of the summits became for me the most fundamental example of the Earth's bunched shoulders and the Earth's naked scalp.

The Cairngorms, sixty miles west of where I lived, defined words like 'highland' and 'mountain' and 'glen' and 'plateau'. The many other gorgeous examples of those that lay to hand – in Glen Clova or Donside or Inverness-shire – were lesser, or junior. The Cairngorms were the great charismatic elders and you came back out of them transformed, in a hum of deep-seated contentment. I camped in the upper glen of the Quoich, under the south-east limb of Beinn a' Bhuird, in a blue October when rutting stags were roaring out of the hill fog like barbarous bassoons; and put a bunch of curly kail from Mrs MacDougall's garden at Inverey into the burn to keep it fresh for cooking with mince and potatoes, over a fire of branches gathered in the silvery ghost of a pinewood felled by the gale of 1893 (or possibly 1879); and shared the plateau of the broad brown mountain above us with a flock of snow buntings that skedaddled over the Alpine mosses like the first blizzard of the winter.

We walked through the Lairig Ghru, twenty-two miles from hostel to hostel (and back the next day), and saw the green haughs of Speyside, far-off through the shallow vee between Carn Eilrig and Creag a' Chalamain, calling us like the promised land; and ate Spam and tinned peaches for our milk-and-honey. We overnighted at the Corrour Bothy under Cairn Toul, swinging along the two-strand wire bridge over the young Dee like drunken gymnasts, then cutting heather with our knives to lay on the hard peat floor and ease our hips. We climbed Ben MacDhui twice on successive April days, footing it effortlessly over the huge shells of re-frozen snow that bridged every burn and hardened every bog. On another more wintry occasion, we reached the MacDhui summit (4296 feet) in a semi-white-out and committed the cardinal blunder of following footsteps in the snow south-south-east, as we thought, to the Sron Riach ridge and the escape route to Glen Luibeg, and followed them and followed them until we checked the compass and saw we had been following ourselves.

As we set out for the Lairig up Glen Luibeg on a day when the west was louring, we met an RAF Mountain Rescue party stretchering down a climber who had fallen hundreds of feet off an ice climb in the Garbh Choire Mor of Braeriach. He had landed on his feet in snow and broken both his legs. It was calm low down and blowing a blizzard in the Lairig – "It's another world round there", said one of the men, his eyes staring and dull. As we took turns with the carrying, we could just see the injured man's face amongst the clothes and blankets. It was pale yellow and blank with morphine, still as a corpse. When we reached Derry Lodge and the press came out to meet us, some of the RAF men were suddenly furious and hurled stones at the photographer.

One summer, in the gently dipping and rising semi-col just east of Einich Cairn, on the way round from Cairn Toul to Braeriach, I came upon what is still the most beautiful thing I have seen, nature's value in its purest essence: a shallow basin in the field of scree, in which water came gradually into focus only because there was a trembling in the few inches of it, the slightest perturbing of the crystal-clear image of the grey gravel that made its bed – Fuaran Dhè, the Wells of Dee. Here the river is secreted by the mountain and at once plunges more than a thousand feet into the Garbh Choire and pours towards Aberdeen. I had been drinking it and washing in it ever since I was born, enjoying it especially when it was peat-brown after heavy rain.

So the means of life flowed from the Cairngorms. They were my bedrock, and my boundary (between our Lowland corner and the Gaelic West), and my marker of the pre-civilised, my type of what came before us, the epitome of the unchanging. Which they are not – the granite crags are wrecks, many of them, like splintered and rotting timbers of colossal stranded ships. When spate water skelps them, it cleaves deep grooves, whose raw sides the plants have a job to re-colonise in this sub-Arctic zone. Unchanging enough, though, their skylines identical before our births and after our deaths, with their look of something that has aged so much, there can be no more ageing in it. As you rise out of Coire Garblach above Glen Feshie and the hoary cranium of Cairn Toul lifts bald and angular across the Mhoine Mhor, the Great Moss, it looks as old as Odin or some other power from that pantheon which feels much closer to me than the Graeco-Roman.

I rang Bill Brooker in the 1980s in the hope that we could climb The Link, in order to write about it for Ken Wilson's book on Very Severe rock-climbs. Bill had put it up with Kenny Grassick, another familiar face from school, whom I hadn't seen for decades. Bill felt that Kenny was more in touch with hard rock these days so in the event it was he and I who made a kind of recce by climbing Pinnacle Face with my eldest son Peter in August 1985. Next year I was back with Kenny under the towering prows of the corrie, after some wet and windy days. We started up Route 1, edged gingerly up the ramp, and retreated baffled by the soapy state of the rock on the short wall below The Springboard. Maybe we would have done better in boots with Tricouni nails, those biting elephant molars that my companions had been wearing on the Black Spout Pinnacle thirty years before. Across the Spout Kenny and I ambled up the Buttress, to have something to show for the long walk in. On the way back down to Fox's Well he kept sitting down on rocks 'for a breather', feeling 'off colour' and 'not himself'. Within the year he had died of leukaemia.

I should have been with them in the mountains in my teens. Held back by shyness, studiousness and unnerving parental pressure, I had missed the sort of chance that comes just once. And yet ... and yet ... the Cairngorms were still there, they hadn't lost any stature to speak of, fugitive sunrays through cloud-dapple still lit their slopes and made a long rise seven miles away look as though you could reach it in half an hour. In July 1990 I walked off round Cairn Gorm with Bill from the top of the ski-lift, and as I followed him down the Coire Raibert path into the great trench of Loch Avon and once again the place enfolded me, cradling me, I didn't let on that I was weeping tears for the youth I should have had.

Across the loch a burn zigzagged down the tawny mountainside in a fierce bolt like white lightning. On all sides the limbs and heads of the bens lay calmly, uneventfully, assuring us that nothing seismic or desperate had happened or would happen here for many millions of years. The clouds were dry and high and bluish-grey like goose-down, the very look of July in Aberdeenshire. We were making for one of Bill and Kenny's classic routes, The Talisman on Creagan a' Choire Etchachan. After an hour's steady climbing up from Loch Avon, over the col past Loch Etchachan and into Coire Etchachan ('corrie of great space'), we off-loaded our sacks where a buttress sprang out of the northernmost slope of Derry Cairngorm and rose for three hundred and fifty feet, as hard and clean as steel to the touch.

From the guidebooks, always a mixed blessing, I knew that the climb started up a 'short crack', on which they spent few words. The first moves up it were like trying to *wade* in rock. A huge recumbent flake is propped against the buttress proper. The fissure between them was obviously what to use. I stuck my left foot crossways into it, knowing it would lodge, hoisted my right one towards the shelf made by the flake, and . . . nothing happened. My foot sank into the crack, and in and in – my other one couldn't quite hook onto the top – I was half-riding an obdurate stone steed, or rather I was slumping back off it in a sweat of frustration. There must be *something*. I braced my left foot hard, pressed sideways on it and . . . it kept disappearing into that narrow, seemingly bottomless shadow.

Whoever set this up for our delectation knew exactly how wide the thing should be to look perfect for our use while denying us any help at all. The stone steed waited patiently while I mounted and slithered and recoiled and tried to make a sort of eight-foot standing jump onto its long-suffering haunches. In the end I grasped the left-hand edge in a horizontal lay-away and pulled, and pulled and pulled – it was like trying to haul a goods train with your bare hands. As my strength drained into the rock, my body rose slowly-slowly. Gravity seemed ten times its normal drag. At the end of it all I floundered onto the flake top like a beached walrus. After that the real climbing began.

It was a joy. It was like singing an aria that lasted for two hours without a break – no repetitions, no bum notes – an unstoppable, melodious upward-pour. The great leaning shield of the traverse slab is seamed with lateral cracks, their lower lips rounded, not too slippery, fairly asking the edges of your feet to sense and sidle with the delicacy of a snail's horns. The angle is comfortable; it's easing us into the body of the mountain. Kenny, who had originally led this pitch, must have felt like whooping and laughing as the massive jigsaw puzzle fitted together piece by piece.

Suddenly the picture completes itself. Beyond its edge there is nothing, or rather, there are the slopes of Sgor an Lochain Uaine a mile away, speckled with boulders, a handsome sight, of no interest to us at this minute. At our feet the crag drops so sheer that its face is invisible. This gulf creates a slightly dizzy vacancy on our left hand for the next hour or two. The crest of the buttress juts above us like a well-muscled torso. Bill and Kenny *knew*, as they looked up at it, that a gem of a route was theirs for the getting.

Everything centres now, like the converging sections of a dartboard, on the 'awkward corner' forty feet above us. I've been reading about it for twelve years, in Ken Wilson's *Classic Rock*. The bones of the crest grind inwards, making two jaws like a giant's gums mumbling, or the nebs of a pair of pliers, or twin millstones set on edge. We are the grist – we have to squeeze through there. I move up, feet clinging as firmly as buckies to the sloping shelves and little floors of this beautiful granite structure. From immediately below, the squeeze looks quite as daunting as it does in those two photos in *Classic Rock*. It overhangs. The converging plates of it are splayed too much for chimneying. The join at the back is too flared for jamming – apart from the fact that if you did slot your hand in there, you'd need a fifteen-foot telescopic left arm to keep it lodged as you shinned up the right-hand wall.

Nothing for it but to cram some body into the narrows and edge upwards while looking for holds on the wall. There aren't any. Reach for the top. It's too far . . . My memory of how I managed it can do no better than a blurred image of shrugging and flexing like some slug or worm. I think I remember a little vertical kerb to push against with the right foot. It isn't in the photos. Before this improbable system of levers and balances gave way, I reached my right-hand fingers over the top at their fullest stretch and found a providential lip. It was rounded, it was shallow; it was just enough.

I was never in the least scared, in spite of the near instability of it all, the drop on both sides, the absence of runners between Bill and myself some forty feet below. It was his presence that did it. He was at home here. He had never come to grief in all those years of rocky and icy exploration, with minimal protection-runners, often in cold and greasy conditions. Amidst all this exposure, this manoeuvring up unsunned greyish and brownish ribs and buttresses and cracked granite bones, I felt happed in familiarity and friendship. The depth of the past, personal, historical, geological, was like a solid atmosphere around me and under my feet. Nothing could go wrong. An unbroken series of stepping-stones had led us to this point, and would lead on across the black waters ahead of us.

That day went on and on, because of the long light less than three weeks after midsummer at a latitude of 57° north and because we were tapping into more than forty years' acquaintance with these mountains, more than fifty with each other. We had been climbing with our rucksacks on. Now, after another hundred feet of pulling up the crest, sometimes stepping down onto small ledges on the right-hand face just for the hell of it, we walked off at the top of the buttress and set our course west, then north-by-west, for the rim of the Cairn Lochan corries and the way back down and round to Coire Cas.

We had finished the climb at over three thousand feet and needed to gain little more than seven hundred and fifty in our two- or three-mile stravaig amongst the gravelly uplands between Loch Avon and the Lairig. We contoured above Loch Etchachan, a broad plate of greenslate rasped by the cool easterly, and crossed the wee burn that flows out of a lochan on the lip of Coire Sputan Dearg. It gurgled under a surviving roof of winter snow and reappeared four hundred and fifty feet below on the verge of the loch. Around us was essence of Cairngorm, the plateau which Nan Shepherd calls 'a single mountain, the fissures and deep descents no more than eddies on the plateau surface.' The broad planes of it tilt this way, tilt that way, the waters gather and are tipped towards the Dee or towards the Spey. The grainy surfaces that swell around you, olive and oatmeal and jade, draw you in and surround you so completely that they become like the inner surfaces of your own head, the folds of your own brain. You never want to leave.

We were going at a kind of fast stroll, as the pigeon-coloured clouds began to flush with the setting of the sun, and talking continuously. How do you describe good talk? Of course it was about old climbing friends. Kenny Grassick, who had remembered me as one of Them, one of the prefects. Graham Nicol, who did great things with Patey – I remembered him as a sulky wee boy who walked along beside the gymnasium hitting his fist against the granite wall. Gordon Lilley, another Aberdeen pioneer, who had married my one-time sister-in-law. And it was about marrying and having children and not getting any younger, and how I had missed the climbing boat as a young man and why Bill had never gone to the Himalaya . . . I was in the midst of fieldwork for a book about great rocks and Bill recommended the tor on Ben Avon called Clach Ban, the Woman Stone, where women used to come from far away to sit in the rounded neuks and ensure an easy confinement. He also repeated the explanation he had given me five years before on Lochnagar of how the 'crumpet formation' of those tors and the paps on Lochnagar had evolved their layered and thick-lipped shapes.

Such rambling rock-talk made the walking feel like gliding. We trudged effortlessly down and up shallow gullies and across fields of old snow darkened round the edges by grains of heather and peat. The sunset clouds were turning from vermilion to burnt orange to apricot to old gold as the last light came slanting through like a furnace door flung open and the silhouette of Carn Eilrig between the Lairig and Gleann Einich made a perfect triangle against the golden dazzle. We could just see our footholds as we stepped steeply down into Coire an Sneachda. From the cauldron of shadow below us a bird was chirruping and Bill identified it as a male snow bunting. Minutes later we were wading through the heather hummocks on the corrie floor and a tousle-headed youth was coming towards us, laden with camping gear, weaving a zigzag course with the help of a pine branch. "Great mountains, man," he burbled dozily. "Like, what's *up* there? I mean, should I go *up* there?" A cold night was darkening over the 4000-foot plateau with its thawing snow-bridges and drops down massive cliffs. Bill advised him pressingly to turn back and stay low. He gave us a carefree "Okay, okay. See you around . . ." and headed on up the mountain.

Bill had been using a telescopic walking stick for balance, especially as he waded shin-deep through the Feith Buidhe where it flows into Loch Avon. For a year or two he had been bothered by a 'pinched nerve' in his lower back which gave him a bad time as he crossed broken ground. The day after The Talisman we came back up to the northern corries with Bill Birkett from Cumbria to climb Savage Slit on Coire an Lochain, a magnificent two-hundred-foot joint between towering faces of horizontally cracked granite, first climbed at the very end of the War. You can bridge at your ease all the way up the beautiful ladder. As I looked down I saw that Bill was having to contort himself in bunched-up back-and-foot positions. His bad back was destabilising him. A year later his condition was finally diagnosed: motor neurone disease. The Talisman and Savage Slit were his last real rock-climbs.

Mind Has Mountains

Allt an Lochain Uaine

At the Burn of the Green Tarn
I was staying a time
And though the place was cold
My dwelling was wonderfully warm.
Though winds from the north came on me
And snow fast-drifting from the height,
The Burn of the Green Tarn
Sent me to sleep with its sound.

My bonny-haired girl,*
Do not be so gloomy or scowling.
Although I go among strangers
I will come home if I am alive,
And when the antlered stag
Is blustering in the glen,
I would not give the taste of your kiss
For the treasure of the Indies.

Night is on me, alone
And living in the glen,
In my little bothy of the rocks
Where you can hear fawns chattering.
On my own, I heard
A voice under my head
Telling me to mind
That men were after me in the glen.

I awoke in alarm
And lifted up my head.
Every tuft of the clothing
I pulled tightly round my shoulders.
The Colonel's Daughter was above me,
She was successful every time,
And she said, "Don't be afraid –
If you must flee do not be slow."

I traversed every burn
From Lui to Carn a' Mhaim.
I watched each one of them
In case there were men in it,
And before the sun rose in the sky
And before it showed on a single hill,
At that moment I knew suddenly
That the Fox was in the glen.**

I reasoned aloud
And I listened to every burn
As they answered each other
Although they had no words at all.
I spoke to my Ruler
Who gave burns from the hardness of the bens.
With the help of the Man who was crucified
I will not be taken into custody.

*The bard's rifle, known as the Colonel's Daughter – a gift from Col. Grant of
Rothiemurchus. **The Earl of Mar's foresters.

Uilleam Rynuie/William Smith.
translated from the Gaelic by Adam Watson (adapted by David Craig)

The Key to a Fragile Silence

I have heard silence only once in my life. I think of it as my life's one sacred moment. It happened in the Cairngorms, far out into the Mhoine Mhor, the Great Moss, a high and undulating plateau land where great winds shout among the rooftops of Scotland.

Here, between 3000 and 4000 feet, is the Arctic heart of the Cairngorms, a landscape without limit under skies which seem to overlap it on all sides, like Orkney heaved up out of its ocean. And like Orkney, it is a place of flattening winds, but the day of the silence, I walked in nothing but the softest breeze.

I was climbing with a friend, the writer David Craig, and we were suddenly aware in the same instant that our feet made the only sound in the landscape. The wind had gone, and its going stopped us dead. Then we heard it – nothing.

No sound. No shred of wind. No whisper of it round a rock or through a tuft of grass, no small tug in an ear. Nothing. No bird call. No deer gutturals, no sheep bleat, no dog bark, no aircraft drone. No fall of water, neither trickle on rock nor slap on shore. No cataract, no single syllable of water. We were too far out on the Great Moss to hear anything other than the Moss's own sounds, and for a few seconds it offered none at all.

I said: "Listen!"

I regret the word, for it besmirched the silence, yet it had the effect of making me listen harder, and the harder I listened, the more vast the silence, the more acute that wondrous, symbolic nothing, a mountain heartbeat, or a glimpse of nature asleep.

Then, the faintest sound I ever remember, a flake of a thing, audible only because it fell, the flight speech of wild geese. We scanned the sky but the Cairngorms' way with unfathomable scale defeated us. How high do you look when you are standing at 3500 feet and a skein of geese of all raucous things reaches you from above as soft as a sliver of a sigh? We found them at last, crossing the mountains at about 7,000 feet, flying fragments of their Arctic. I wonder what they made of Davie and me, tinily inching across our own single Arctic survivor, a landscape still capable – for all man's intrusions – of startling susceptible mortals with silence.

We have, between us, more than sixty years of wandering wild places. We could remember no such silence. Perhaps it occurs in mid-Sahara, or the Australian outback. Mostly when it occurs at all, it will be the preserve of the Arctic. And therein lies the plight of the Cairngorms. It is an Arctic place in the hands of people who think they live a thousand miles south of the Arctic Circle.

The governing characteristic of Arctic places is fragility. That knowledge, allied to the status of the Cairngorms as a unique landform in our midst, should be enough to persuade any self-esteeming society that here is a place to revere, not for crude assessments of its commercial prospects but for its own sake. Here, as surely as in mid-ocean or tropical rainforest, is a place where natural forces work at their extremities. The dignified response from a society which cares about where it lives would be to stand back . . . give nature its head, wonder and admire.

Instead, its huge estates are bought and sold on whims, serious nature conservation intent has been either discouraged or conspired against. Landowning practice locks the landscape into timewarps of anti-nature, its landowners' complacency and the meddling of local and national politics. Over much of the mountain massif, nature is in retreat. Yet how eagerly it would advance if it were given so much as half a chance! It takes considerable energies and vast resources to keep nature in check in a landscape as natural as the Cairngorms. It seems no expense is spared to fankle nature, to batten it down, close it in, stamp it out.

For example: by any reasonable comparison of what has been in the past and what exists now, Glen Feshie is derelict, dying on its feet. Yet the means to save it, to resuscitate nature and let it live and breathe again was on offer three or four years ago, a bid for ownership by the Royal Society for the Protection of Birds (RSPB) and the John Muir Trust (JMT).

The RSPB has demonstrated at Abernethy that it can unite its own energies and resources to the breadth of its imagination. Abernethy is a liberated landscape. The John Muir Trust is still new to the business of conservation-based landownership, but it could have learned a lot very quickly from direct association with the RSPB in a Cairngorms setting.

What these two organisations have going for them is a purity of purpose, that and an accountability to a membership of real people. In the RSPB's case, that membership is approaching one million real people. The alliance of the RSPB and the JMT was a solution to the ills of Glen Feshie on a plate. If the Government wanted to demonstrate it had the well being of the natural environment at heart, here was a political opportunity fallen into its lap, as manna from heaven.

But the National Heritage Memorial Fund rebuffed a modest request and the path was smoothed for the mysterious Will Woodland Trust to buy the estate, with pious pledges from anonymous spokesmen. The trustees are three London lawyers whose ignorance of what it is to be a trustee of a landscape such as Glen Feshie has been breathtakingly demonstrated. It is a naïve fool who believes anything other than that landowning interests wanted to ensure that conservation principles did not dictate the future of Glen Feshie. There are few naïve fools left among those who fight for the future of the Cairngorms.

When the National Trust for Scotland (NTS) was given twice as much money as the RSPB and JMT had sought, this time to buy the huge Mar

Lodge estate, any lingering doubts were banished. The NTS has a record of mountain estate management which is less than exemplary, but its links with the Scottish Landowners Federation and the Conservative Government run deep.

What the Government has done to subjugate all hopes of serious Cairngorms-wide progress is to hamstring its agency, Scottish Natural Heritage (SNH), with impotent dead weights of bureaucracy. In the recent *Frontline Scotland* programme, which tried to unravel the Cairngorms' many controversies, the most insipid contribution came from the mouth of SNH's director, ending with a plaintive "What's the rush?" defence of the indefensible.

The Government has also created the Cairngorms Partnership, a laborious talking shop of all the mountain's vested interests, a forum which guarantees that radical voices will be shouted down, that radical solutions will be suffocated by the perpetual quest for compromise.

Compromise has given the Cairngorms what it has now, which is insidious dereliction. The devastating power of the compromise culture is seen in the response of conservation groups to the preposterous proposal for a funicular railway on the Cairn Gorm ski slopes: not a railway, a gondola!

You can hear the fearful voices at work. "We mustn't be seen to be negative. We must make a position contribution. Propose a less damaging alternative . . . damage limitation, that's the answer."

No, it's not the answer. Not in the Cairngorms. Not in that priceless fragment of the Arctic! Not in that harbourer of silence! Not in the most precious landscape we know! Damage limitation will not do. Only restoration will do. Healing the landscape of all its wounds – that is the only cause worth fighting for in the Cairngorms, conservation on a scale conservationists have not yet cared to contemplate.

The author of the best piece of nature writing I have ever read, Aldo Leopold, wrote in his book *A Sand County Almanac*: 'The practices we now call conservation are, to a large extent, local alleviations of biotic pain. They are necessary, but they must not be confused with cures.' It is cures we should be seeking in the Cairngorms.

The implication of Leopold's truism is that there is an immensity of difference between conservation and cure. In the Cairngorms, uniquely (that word again! It is nowhere more truly and worthily applicable than in the Cairngorms), it is the immensity of difference which matters.

There is nothing like the landscape of the Cairngorms, and skiing should play no part in it, none at all, and neither should the pot-shot priorities of Victorian landowners.

The cure for the Cairngorms lies in removing both these, for they are the unquestionable obstacles towards the natural regeneration of every indigenous habitat, the factors which act contrary to the well-being of the mountain massif, the forces of anti-nature.

Cloud cuckoo land, right? Unhinged from the real world, right?

Or, as a Scottish Landowners Federation spokesman said recently: "There is an awful lot of chasing moonbeams among conservationists in the Cairngorms. Things aren't really that bad."

The voice of reason, delivered as always in cut-glass, public-school tones. It is meant to reassure us. It does not reassure nature. And neither does a gondola. The only thing which holds conservation in check in the Cairngorms is the limit of its own ambition. If it includes a gondola in its definition of acceptable conservation practice, then it is certainly not interested in cures.

The search for a cure begins with the removal of all skiing from the Cairngorms, the closing of Cairn Gorm for, say, a hundred years, which should be long enough to let it heal.

Skiing can flourish in many places in Scotland, but as long as it is a component of what the Cairngorms landscape has become, its commercial ambitions will grow and grow and nature and its silences in the Cairngorms will wither.

The chairman of the Cairn Gorm Company defended the funicular railway recently with the familiar pronouncement that the economy of the Highlands is "yoked to tourism". It is a half-truth, and if it is truer now than it used to be, that is no cause for celebration, for it is the most thoughtless and demeaning of industries at its worst. And its worst lies perilously close to the foot of the Cairn Gorm ski slopes . . .

Yet conservation on a Cairngorms-wide scale offers untold employment prospects, recruiting from a local workforce, teaching real skills, creating jobs for all time which are not dependent on the weather. The only reason why there has been no study of the prospects for yoking the economy of the Highlands from Speyside to Deeside to conservation is because vested interests fear it.

But it is the way forward. A Scottish parliament with powers to establish that in some places (and the Cairngorms is the top of that short list) land management means nature conservation as first priority; and a conservation movement which dares beyond its wildest dreams . . . None of these things is beyond us.

A cure of the Cairngorms is within our grasp, as is a sanctuary for its silences.

Jim Crumley

Beside Loch Eanaich

Beside Loch Eanaich, this July day, a profusion of violets blossomed, some of them of unusual size. July violets in the high corries are common; in the glens they are rare, but in 1923 summer was more than a month later than the average, and spring and full summer came together to the hills.

In the corrie known as Coire nan Each, or the Corrie of the Horses, a number of hinds with their calves were grazing or quietly resting. Some of the young calves were playing together, while the mothers looked on approvingly. Above Coire nan Each the stalking path winds, and then emerges on the edge of that extensive table-land known as An Mhoine Mhor, or the Great Moss. Beside Fuaran Diòtach (the Luncheon Springs) my companions and I lunched, at the edge of a snow-field. By now the clouds were lowering, and the mutterings of distant thunder were heard to the west and south. At 3,000 feet the heat continued as oppressive as ever.

The plateau was still plentifully streaked with snow, and the young grass scarcely showed green. Many ptarmigan scurried around us, intent on decoying us from their newly hatched chicks; from a little peaty knoll a golden plover fluted mournfully. High above Loch Eanaich a golden eagle sailed.

The sky had now brightened, and it seemed as though the thunder had gone, but as we crossed the plateau below Loch nan Cnapan (the Loch of the Knolls) the skies once more became gloomy, rain began to fall, and soon changed into large lumps of half-melted ice. These lumps were jagged, and not rounded as hailstones; perhaps they had been partially melted in the heated air during their rapid descent. In a few moments the plateau was almost white. Suddenly the gloom was rent by a blinding flash of jagged forked lightning, and in a couple of seconds the thunder crashed more deafeningly than I have ever before heard it. In great echoes from hill to hill it rolled, and at once the plateau was alive with the flutter of white wings as ptarmigan rose all around us and flew this way and that in great terror and confusion. My collie dog Dileas, already depressed by the gloom and falling ice, on the clap of thunder staggered forward as though shot; she was henceforth the most miserable object. And yet on the skyline a herd of stags continued calmly to feed!

The storm now momentarily increased in violence. The lightning was dazzling, the thunder extraordinarily close to us. And the rain – it is impossible to describe the floods of water that were poured out on that great mountain plateau. It was as though one were standing beneath a shower bath, and the torrential rain as it struck the ground rebounded to a height of a couple of feet so that a low mist of spray lay upon all the plateau. But worse was still to come. From Glen Giusachan to the south a solid wall of water was now seen approaching. It reached and deluged us; through this cloud-burst it was scarcely possible to see two hundred yards. The lightning was awe inspiring, the thunder one continuous roar; the only comfort we could take was that the rain was warm.

The downpour gradually lessened, and suddenly to the westward Ben Alder and Ben Lawers could be seen in clear sunshine. From the top of Coire Dhondail one looked into a seething cauldron of mist – swirling eddying mist – and torrential rain through which the lightning flickered. Loch Eanaich was almost immediately beneath us, yet was invisible in the storm. Gradually the clouds lifted, and the loch, and the dark precipices of Sgoran Dubh behind it, showed dimly. The face of Sgoran Dubh an hour previous had been waterless; now innumerable burns foamed milky here as they rushed impetuously to the loch below. Such a scene of magnificent grandeur as one may see but once in a lifetime; once seen, it is treasured as a priceless gift of the high hills.

As we looked into the corrie a hen ptarmigan rose almost at our feet. She seemed unmindful of our presence, and, accompanied by her seven downy chicks, walked slowly away, happy at having preserved her family through the perils of the storm.

Soon the midsummer sun shone out once more upon the plateau where we stood. It drew from the many plants of the cushion pink – then in full flower – a delightful scent, and the whole hill seemed refreshed and rejuvenated by the warm, almost tropical, rain. Far westward one saw the distant hills of the Atlantic seaboard – Ben Nevis, Ben Cruachan, the peaks of Knoydart – stand out in fine weather. We heard later that the great thunderstorm had not touched them. All about us ptarmigan with their young sunned themselves and dried their matted feathers, and upon the plateau the effects of the storm quickly disappeared.

But when we descended to Loch Eanaich we found that, severe as had been the storm on the hill-tops, it had been even more violent in Glen Eanaich below. Although the rain had ceased some hours, each small burn was still a raging torrent. Lightning had struck the precipice of Sgoran Dubh. It had sliced away a strip of rock thirty to forty feet in height as cleanly as one cuts a cake with a knife. In a gully beneath the 'cut' great blocks of stone were lying in confusion.

Loch Eanaich, acting as a reservoir and a filter, had prevented the Beanaidh from rising to the same extent as other streams, and it was only when we reached the lower bothy of Glen Eanaich that we realized the force of the rains. Beanaidh Bheag, the tributary of the Beanaidh that has its source partly in Coire an Lochain and partly in Coire Beanaidh, was the colour of pea soup. But the bulk of the flood water had gone before us, and it was thus somewhat of a shock to find that a small burn which crosses the road a little way below the bothy had risen to such an extent that it had carried away its bridge! It had scoured a channel fully six times the width of its original course, and down this channel a great volume of turgid water was still hurrying, so that one had to wade to the knee to cross it.

A few hundred yards farther down the glen another wee burn crosses the road before joining the Beanaidh. Some three hundred yards west of the present road, but close beside the old track, which in places may still be seen traversing the glen, a very old Scots fir grows beside this burn. It is called Craobh Tillidh, or the Tree of the Return, and received its name in the old days when a summer population lived at the head of Glen Eanaich, and when the stirks, and the cows with their calves, were driven up a few days before the people themselves went to the shielings. The herdsman accompanied the animals as far as the Tree of the Return. From here the beasts, knowing the road from former summers, were able to continue the journey by themselves, and the herdsman returned to Rothiemurchus. The old fir must be centuries old, yet it can never have had so narrow an escape as during this great thunderstorm. The small stream beside which it stands had risen to a raging torrent, for a cloud-burst had evidently struck the hill only a few yards from the tree. The old fir had miraculously escaped, for beside it heather, earth and large boulders had been dislodged and swept down upon the road, where hundreds of tons of debris had been deposited. Opposite, upon Carn Eilerig, lightning had struck the hill, tearing a hole and uprooting every tree around.

At several points the Beanaidh had changed its course, and the torrent was flowing across long heather. Through one of these new channels the burn still flows (January 1925).

The scene was thus one of devastation even before we entered the forest, but once in the wood, we looked upon havoc immeasurably greater. In the upper part of the glen we had seen the evening sun burn upon the precipices and glistening snow-fields of Coire Ruadh, and a sky of deepest blue replace the storm-clouds, but now, as if Nature repented of her fury and sought to hide her handiwork, a dense mist crept up the course of the Beanaidh, rendering still more unreal the scene that greeted our eyes. Hundreds of grown fir trees had been uprooted by the torrent of the Beanaidh. They now lay piled up on either bank, or stranded in shoal water. Many boulders had been rolled down the riverbed, and had rubbed the trees and stripped them of their bark. From their weather-beaten appearance they might have been uprooted years before. And yet that very morning they had stood, erect and full of vitality, beside a stream that had then no menace for them. In places the trees had been heaped up in disorder across the burn, forming barriers against which the eager waters pressed.

At that point of the stream known formerly as Caigeann Beanaidh but now as Windy Corner the steep banks of the stream had been scooped out, and the rocks and gravel, bereft of all vegetation, showed up strangely. Even as I stood upon it the river bank commenced to slide stealthily towards the raging flood, bearing with it bushes and full-grown firs and alders. Fortunately the motion ceased as quietly as it had commenced, and the trees still stood erect and unharmed.

Seton Gordon, from *The Cairngorm Hills of Scotland*, 1925

This changing of focus in the eye, moving the eye itself when looking at things that do not move, deepens one's sense of outer reality. Then static things may be caught in the very act of becoming. By so simple a matter, too, as altering the position of one's head, a different kind of world may be made to appear. Lay the head down, or better still, face away from what you look at, and bend with straddled legs till you see your world upside down. How new it has become! From the close-by sprigs of heather to the most distant fold of the land, each detail stands erect in its own validity. In no other way have I seen of my own unaided sight that the earth is round. As I watch, it arches its back, and each layer of landscape bristles – though *bristles* is a word of too much commotion for it. Details are no longer part of a grouping in a picture of which I am the focal point, the focal point is everywhere. Nothing has reference to me, the looker. This is how the earth must see itself.

So I looked slowly across the Coire Loch, and began to understand that haste can do nothing with these hills. I knew when I had looked for a long time that I had hardly begun to see. So with Loch Avon. My first encounter was sharp and astringent, and has crystallised forever for me some innermost inaccessibility. I had climbed all six of the major summits, some of them twice over, before clambering down into the mountain trough that holds Loch Avon. This loch lies at an altitude of some 2300 feet, but its banks soar up for another fifteen hundred. Indeed farther, for Cairn Gorm and Ben MacDhui may be said to be its banks. From the lower end of this mile and a half gash in the rock, exit is easy but very long. One may go down by the Avon itself, through ten miles as lonely and unvisited as anything in the Cairngorms, to Inchrory; or under the Barns of Bynack to the Caiplich Water. But higher up the loch there is no way out, save by scrambling up one or other of the burns that tumble from the heights: except that, above the Shelter Stone, a gap opens between the hills to Loch Etchachan, and here the scramble up is shorter.

The inner end of this gash has been howked straight from the granite. As one looks up from below, the agents would appear mere splashes of water, whose force might be turned aside by a pair of hands. Yet above the precipices we have found in one of these burns pools deep enough to bathe in. The water that pours over these grim bastions carries no sediment of any kind in its precipitate fall, which seems indeed to distil and aerate the water so that the loch far below is sparkling clear. This narrow loch has never, I believe, been sounded. I know its depth, though not in feet.

I first saw it on a cloudless day of early July. We had started at dawn, crossed Cairn Gorm at about nine o'clock, and made our way by the Saddle to the lower end of the loch. Then we idled up the side, facing the gaunt corrie, and at last, when the noonday sun penetrated directly into the water, we stripped and bathed. The clear water was at our knees, then at our thighs. How clear it was only this walking into it could reveal. To look through it was to discover its own properties. What we saw under water had a sharper clarity than what we saw through air. We waded on into the brightness, and the width of the water increased, as it always does when one is on or in it, so that the loch no longer seemed narrow, but the far side was a long way off. Then I looked down; and at my feet there opened a gulf of brightness so profound that the mind stopped. We were standing on the edge of a shelf that ran some yards into the loch before plunging down to the pit that is the true bottom. And through that inordinate clearness we saw to the depth of the pit. So limpid was it that every stone was clear.

I motioned to my companion, who was a step behind, and she came, and glanced as I had down the submerged precipice. Then we looked into each other's eyes and again into the pit. I waded slowly back into shallower water. There was nothing that seemed worth saying. My spirit was as naked as my body. It was one of the most defenceless moments of my life.

I do not think it was the imminence of personal bodily danger that shook me. I had not then, and have not in retrospect, any sense of having just escaped a deadly peril. I might of course have over-balanced and been drowned; but I do not think I would have stepped down unawares. Eye and foot acquire in rough walking a co-ordination that makes one distinctly aware of where the next step is to fall, even while watching sky and land. This watching, it is true, is of a general nature only; for attentive observation the body must be still. But in a general way, in country that is rough, but not difficult, one sees where one is and where one is going at the same time . . . I do not think I was in much danger just then of drowning, nor was fear the emotion with which I stared into the pool. That first glance down had shocked me to a heightened power of myself, in which even fear became a rare exhilaration: not that it ceased to be fear, but fear itself, so impersonal, so keenly apprehended, enlarged rather than constricted the spirit.

The inaccessibility of this loch is part of its power. Silence belongs to it. If jeeps find it out, or a funicular railway disfigures it, part of its meaning will be gone. The good of the greatest number is not here relevant. It is necessary to be sometimes exclusive, not on behalf of rank or wealth, but of those human qualities that can apprehend loneliness.

Nan Shepherd, from *The Living Mountain*, 1977

The Talisman: The First Ascent

Talisman: a charm, a thing capable of working wonders ... and of benefiting its possessor. (Concise Oxford Dictionary)

Coire Etchachan lies tucked into the eastern flank of Ben Macdui between the boulder strewn domes of Derry Cairngorm and the massive hulk of Beinn Mheadhoin. It opens into the upper part of the narrow glacial trench of Glen Derry and is traditionally reached by following the path along the old droving route of the Lairig an Laoigh across the grassy flats of the glen and branching left when it starts the ascent to the pass. An alternative and shorter but more arduous approach is from the north using one of the routes from the Cairngorm Car Park into the Loch Avon basin. From the head of Loch Avon it goes by the path rising steeply to Loch Etchachan and following the outlet stream down into the corrie. The northern and southern sides of Coire Etchachan have some rock outcrop but are of little climbing interest. It is the headwall forming the centrepiece of the western side which draws the eye. Here there is a face of granite four hundred feet high, with two big square-cut gullies and a line of overhangs ascending from left to right. These are set between two dominating features, a steep face of smooth red granite on the right – The Crimson Slabs, and a huge, broad-based buttress on the left – The Bastion.

In the Cairngorms rock climbing had been much slower to develop than in Glencoe or on Nevis largely because Cairngorm granite had been libelled in early guidebooks as unsuited to climbing – being rounded, loose, unreliable and frequently vegetated. To some extent these accusations were justified in the early days when climbing was mainly in the gullies. It was different out on the buttresses and faces where the rock was much better and often excellent. With exceptions such as The Mitre Ridge on Beinn a Bhuird and Eagle Ridge on Lochnagar very little climbing development of this kind occurred until the late 1940s and early 1950s when corrie after corrie was discovered to contain rewarding climbing opportunities. Although Coire Etchachan lies on one of the most frequented routes to Ben Macdui rock climbing exploration here did not begin until 1949, continuing through the 1950s until all the main features had been climbed. The Bastion was among the first to be visited and by 1953 had no less than four different routes. The granite rocks of The Bastion are more broken to the left and become more compact further right, where the density of ribs and grooves increases until the buttress forms a massive edge. This plunges in a smooth wall of slabs into a big gully called The Corridor. The rock structure of the buttress is reflected by the progressive rise in standard of difficulty of the early Bastion climbs from left to right, Mod., Diff., Mild Severe, Severe. The latest one to be made used what seemed to be the final line of weakness and was given the over-ambitious name of Corridor Edge, later changed to Red Scar Route when the edge itself became The Talisman three years later.

By 1956 the nailed boots traditional for climbing in the Cairngorms were beginning to give way to more modern footwear. It was late June and the weather was perfect. Ken Grassick and I had enjoyed a new route on the steep face of The Black Spout Pinnacle of Lochnagar only the previous weekend, The Link, and had discovered for ourselves that lightweight vibram-soled boots opened the way to all sorts of unlikely places as long as the granite was dry. We stood at the Etchachan Hut wondering whether to go over to the Crimson Slabs or to the Corridor edge of the Bastion and chose the latter. Perhaps because it looked as if it would offer the kind of exploratory climbing we liked best, working our way up varied rock without any clear expectation of what lay ahead.

We stood below and studied the cliff. The edge of The Bastion, sharply defined by the slabby Corridor wall, swept down from above to a point about a hundred feet above the widening mouth of the gully.

Here the edge was undercut by a huge overhang, which seemed to us an impassable barrier (although it would be penetrated by an 'E' Grade Direct Start in 1981). However the wall itself took the form of a great slab, well seamed by cracks, and might be traversed keeping above the lip of the overhang. At the gully entrance two masses of rock leaned against the overhanging wall to form a giant flake crack in two parts with a platform in between. We chose this as our start and scrambled onto the platform to rope up. In those simpler days before harnesses and racks this involved no more than tying bowlines around our waists with our two 120 foot 'threequarter' laid nylon ropes and arranging a few slings with karabiners (best ex-WD) just in case we encountered the odd rock spike to provide a runner. Our rope technique was not nearly as sophisticated as that employed further south and runners were infrequent. Pitches were therefore kept short except in winter when time was of the essence. As was the usual practice on unexplored Cairngorm rock we had a couple of rock pegs against an absence of natural belays for advance or retreat. I also carried an eight-inch piece of thick aluminium angle which would provide a secure main belay (I claimed), if driven into turf. This had already been in action and given me a sense of security although admittedly the turf had been frozen on that occasion. Anyway I liked to have it with me as a kind of talisman.

Grassick habitually enjoyed a tin of fruit before a climb and I was always ready to support him in this harmless eccentricity, provided he carried it, of course. I seem to remember it was pineapple on this occasion, decorated with what I took to be a Hawaiian damsel sunning herself on the empty tin, and musing on how nice it would be to be there instead of here in Coire Etchachan with a lot of hard work looming above, Grassick grunted his disapproval and launched himself at the crack.

This first pitch wasn't complicated but it was quite strenuous as the crack was wide enough to accept the whole of the left leg while the right foot scrabbled for purchase on the flawless outer face of the great block. It wasn't steep but jamming the left foot and knee to make progress was awkward and the sweat was beginning to flow by the time forty feet had been covered and a ledge at the top of the block reached. When I rejoined Ken I saw that we were now at the lip of the slabby wall. After moving a little to the right I found the slab surface was broken with big holds which led me easily upward to a niche forty feet above. Here a traverse out across the slab seemed possible. The niche gave a stance and the absence of any belay was soon rectified by one of the rock pegs. I brought Ken up and assured him that his traverse out to the crest would look sensational in the photograph I was about to take and that in spite of our exposed position I could hold a double decker bus. Off he went, stitching together the footholds, kicking off lumps of moss and lichen here and there, first over to a little niche, then down a step or two and delicately across a smooth section to reach a small footledge leading to more holds and finally gaining access to a stance, fifty feet away on the crest itself. Here he squatted beneath a small overhang and called for me to follow. When I reached the crest I found that the squat was to make the most of the low-set flake around which the ever-optimistic Grassick had arranged our joint security.

It was an impressive spot, with the crestal rocks undercut about thirty feet below us and rising steeply in cracked slabs and corners to an overhung recess fifty feet above. The sun was just reaching us on our perch and gilding the upper lip of the recess, which was obviously the next objective. I sidled round to the left and found good pulling edges of granite to take me to a heathery ledge, back above the stance and then zigzagging upward by slab and corner to the key recess. Its leaning walls were not high but devoid of the kind of jughandle I require in such situations. I stopped and looked in vain for a belay. There was no turf ledge to speak of. There was, however, a crack, quite a wide crack, so I took out my talisman and tapped in eight inches of aluminium angled security. To this I yoked myself and took in the rope. "Just the sort of move you like," I said, as Ken climbed over me and stepped on my shoulder to have a look over the lip. A heave, a grunt and he was up, and in a few more feet had reached a comfortable ledge with a splendid block belay.

I extracted the belay and thrutched out of the recess to join him in the sunshine. The next thirty feet were easy and we could see that a turfy groove just to the left of the crest led all the way to the top of the buttress. We had no more problems and it was a beautiful day. That groove was to become the line taken on the first winter ascent made by Grassick and Jerry Light nine years in the future. However, on this occasion, it was the crest itself which was to give a proper finish to our route, a hundred feet of clean exposed granite, at first moving crablike on the outer wall as the Corridor yawned hungrily below, then swinging back onto the arête and following this on superb and gradually improving holds to the broken upper rocks and the plateau.

We felt great. The climb we had made had extracted the best from the Bastion and brought the first phase of its exploration to a satisfying conclusion. Others would come later and venture in places that were inaccessible to us but The Talisman had yielded the natural line up that magnificent feature of granite architecture along the edge above the Corridor. Contentedly we wandered along in brilliant sunshine to the shore of Loch Etchachan. Here we sat for a little in the very heart of the Cairngorms, sensing we had been privileged to experience a true intimacy with the mountains.

Bill Brooker

Seen fae the Bivvy

Stewart McGavin

Seen fae the Bivvy

Ben Lawers at nicht
near the tap, sclimman through
'a Perkinje fringe'

yon wee hill
I canna get up it
for the trees

Sgurr nan Gillean
souns I the mist, mair fowk,
on the tourist route

the hare, white
bit jist veesible
on the sna.

Beinn a Bhuird
seen fae the bivvy
dotterel

Stewart McGavin

The Flowers of Ben Lawers

Colin Will

The Flowers of Ben Lawers

It may seem paradoxical, but in the world of immobile plants nothing ever stands still. Landscapes now dominated by heather and bracken were not always so, indeed bracken itself seems to be a hybrid, the result of a chance mating between spores of two separate fern species. Hills that are cursed for being clothed in uniform dark green swathes of spruce were once jacketed in oak and birch and pine, albeit not planted in drained rows. We look at our upland landscapes in Perthshire and Argyll, and think they reflect the natural order of things, an Arcadian Eden, the way things always used to be. Not so, things were never the way they always used to be. Climate has played a large part in these changes, but for really big change you need two other essential ingredients: people and carelessness.

∗ ∗ ∗

As Scotland emerged from the last Ice Age, ten thousand or so years ago, plants colonised the land, establishing communities in sites that best suited them. Low-lying ground was the first to be seeded, and the mountain tops the last. The glaciers left behind bare rock, thick deposits of clay, and outwash deposits of sand and gravel. No soil yet, for that requires the addition of organic material, but the stage was set for the greening of Scotland.

As ice lobes retreated the marginal tundra vegetation extended into newly available niches. Ground-hugging lichens, biochemical crusts, digested the clay particles, dissolving out nutrients to nourish their symbiotic partnerships of fungi and algae. Mosses and liverworts soaked up moisture, forming organic mats of green seasonal flushes where snow and ice allowed. Seeds of the higher plants were blown in, and occasionally took hold, establishing patches of grass, herbs, and stunted bushes. Over hundreds of years, conditions improved; warmer summers enabling plants to put on enough growth to see them through the winters, and to set their seed. Communities of herbs, shrubby plants, and finally trees established and took hold. The early colonisers, suited to the harshest conditions, kept pace with the retreating ice, until the last glaciers melted from the high tops, and left them stranded on our highest mountains, where some yet remain. These patchy remnants of Arctic-Alpine vegetation form a specialist flora that has always fascinated those individuals who relish our mountains.

In the valleys there was a natural succession of plant communities. Fast growing, short-lived birch and hazel scrub, with willow and alder in the wetter ground, were followed eventually by the climax vegetation. Oak and pine woodland, with an understorey of herbaceous plants and grasses, is probably the landscape our earliest ancestors saw first when they left their seashore shell middens and began to move inland. Would these early folk have been interested in visiting the high mountains? We know they sought out high viewpoints in the Lowlands, they left their marks and monuments, but did the mountains mean anything to them? We don't know, possibly we will never know, but like Lewis Grassic Gibbon in *Sunset Song,* we can speculate on their thoughts and feelings: '... he pictured the dark, slow tribes that came drifting across the low lands of the northern seas ... God's children in the morn of time.'

They used the woodlands for building homes, for stabilising tracks through bogs, for bridging streams, for firewood. They fished and hunted, made fences for their beasts, built ovens for pottery, the smelting of ores and the working of bronze. They cleared patches of good ground to grow the first crops. Their impact on the forests was marginal, for stone or bronze axes are limited, and their numbers were small.

Where then did all the trees go? New people arrived in successive waves from continental Europe, to populate the empty islands. The forests went, to clear more land for agriculture, to make ships from oak beams, to make charcoal to feed the iron industry, to clear the slopes for sheep. At first, when things were on a small scale, the pace of deforestation was slow but steady. As ships got bigger, each might take a hundred trees to build, and by the time of the Napoleonic wars, hundreds of ships were built. As the iron-works at Furnace and Bonawe grew, Argyll's oak woods were decimated. As the lowlands of the Northeast and the Central belt were planted to barley and roots, whole forests were picked off. And when the little black-faced sheep were heft to their hillslopes, pine, juniper, birch, rowan and aspen stumped up to pay for woolly jumpers. It wasn't a deliberate decision – 'Let's clear away all the trees!' – it was just the way things happened.

* * *

The Scottish mountains can be grouped botanically, according to their altitude and geology, both of which have profound effects on the vegetation they support. The tops of the Cairngorms form a rocky plateau, snow-covered for most of each year, in which our true Arctic-Alpine communities somehow exist, sheltering from the constant wind, extracting a meagre living from the nutrient-poor acid rocks. The volcanic hills of Western Scotland are made of basalts and gabbros, both alkali-rich, but slow to weather and release their nutrients. The Torridonian mountains of the Northwest Highlands are isolated sandstone peaks, some topped with layers of hard limestone and even harder quartzite – distinctive landforms with their own particular rarities. The Scottish Primrose – *Primula scotica* – grows only on the Durness dolomite.

The richest mountain environments in Scotland are those forming the Central Highlands. The predominant rock-types here are mica-schists, variable in composition. At their heart, the Breadalbane hills contain calc-alkaline rocks which hold onto their minerals less tightly than elsewhere, and have given rise to the unique plant communities of the Lawers range, to the north of Loch Tay. They are the most botanised of Scotland's mountains, and hold some of its most beautiful and rare plants.

Botanical exploration in Scotland is first recorded by the Rev. John Lightfoot, in his *Flora Scotica*, published in 1778. Not too long afterwards George Don, a nurseryman from Forfar, began his own detailed excursions in the 'Caledonian Alps'. It was in the Victorian era that Britain's passion for plants took off, and no Victorian naturalist completed his or her education without a visit to Ben Lawers.

The number of professional botanists has always been small, but the study of plants has been popular among students and amateurs alike. A perfectly natural and worthy ambition to record, study and document our land and its living organisms was the driving force behind the establishment of institutions such as the Geological Survey of Great Britain and several University Departments of Botany and Zoology. In the case of plants, it was obvious early on that there were plants in the mountains that weren't seen elsewhere. Having been seen, they could also be collected, and another species of human carelessness was created.

Plants not only needed to be seen and recorded, they had to be collected, so they could be dried and preserved in 'herbaria' for comparative study. It was common practice in the nineteenth century for botanical students to make their own representative collections of the Scottish flora, and for these herbaria to be marked and assessed. Amateurs too made their own collections, and when they banded together in societies, the scale of collecting grew.

Extract from *Report on the Excursion of the Scottish Alpine Botanical Club to Killin and Loch Awe in 1885.*

Friday 31st July. After an early breakfast, the members of the Club drove to Lawers Inn, where we left our conveyance, and immediately commenced the ascent of Ben Lawers, the eighth highest mountain in Scotland, but undoubtedly the richest in botanical treasures.

The morning being misty, and the grass wet with dew, we made the ascent as far as Lochan a' Chait by the 'old peat road'. On a steep bank on the west side of Lawers Burn we gathered beautiful specimens of *Digitalis* of a cream colour, and some pure white – probably the very bank on which Mr M'Nab, in an excursion with the late Professor Graham in 1839, 'found a beautiful cream-coloured variety of *Digitalis purpurea* (foxglove), a little way above Lawers Inn, by the side of a stream'.

By the time we reached Lochan a' Chait the mist had cleared away, and the day had become exceedingly hot, with a burning sun over our heads. This rendered alpine climbing somewhat uncomfortable, and we were glad occasionally to get under the shade of the rocks, and on our way to the summit we found the large patches of snow most refreshing and cooling. Upwards of twenty patches of snow were observed on this side of the hill, some of these many feet deep, and covering several acres.

The whole party reached the summit in the course of the afternoon, and were rewarded with a magnificent view.

We found most of the good plants known to grow on Ben Lawers, including *Cerastium alpinum; Cerastium latifolium; Sagina linnaei; Potentilla salisburgensis; Saxifraga nivalis; Saxifraga cernua,* one specimen of which was in flower; *Erigeron alpinum* in fine flower; *Trientalis europaea; Myosotis alpestris* (many of the ravines were exquisitely beautiful with this, the prettiest of all our forget-me-nots); *Juncus triglumis; Juncus biglumis; Juncus castaneus; Carex pulla; Cystopteris montana*; and *Aspidium lonchitis*. A plant of the last, with very broad pinnae, was also gathered.

Another excellent find was *Cystopteris montana*, in fine condition, and considerable abundance. It was on Ben Lawers that this beautiful fern was first discovered in Britain in 1836. It has occasionally been gathered since on Ben Lawers, but the station was known only to few, if at all, and certainly it was not known to any member of the Alpine Club.

William Craig. 1885

The collecting continued throughout the century. In the 1848 excursion fifty-three species were collected and on the 1871 trip, again, many of the rare alpine plants of Britain. Many other excursions to Lawers throughout the 1880's and '90's are recorded. I calculate, based on the numbers of excursions, numbers in party, and records of plants, that at least 20,000 specimens of rare plants were removed from Scottish mountains between 1860 and 1900 *by botanists*. To this must be added the (probably larger) numbers taken by students and amateurs. Say 50,000 plants in the period, from populations which were never large, and which are generally slow to reproduce.

Today's generation of botanists cares much more for the objects of their study, and some are involved in conservation projects aimed at restoring our rare plants to their natural habitats. Few of our mountains are free from the depredations of the Black-faced Sheep, however, and there is no point in re-introducing plants unless the sheep are excluded. Ben Lawers has a good example of an 'exclosure' adjacent to the National Trust for Scotland's Visitor Centre. Here, safe from grazing pressure, the natural vegetation is being re-established, and the path winds up through an increasingly diverse and interesting range of unusual sedges, rushes, grasses, ferns, shrubs and herbaceous plants. It will take a few more years before the place returns to its pre-sheep appearance, but it will.

Deer too are another problem in the higher country. When numbers are small they cause less habitat destruction than sheep. Where the stocking rate is too high, however, and they can't browse in the lowlands in winter as they used to, they can overgraze with the best of them. If the return on hill venison remains lower than for the farmed variety, landowners say there's no point in shooting them, and numbers rise inexorably. The 'easy answer' fraternity recommend that we re-introduce wolves to redress the balance, but the wolf is not a stupid animal – it will take sheep as the easier prey, rather than the fleeter deer.

Botanists were in the vanguard of those trying to establish a right of free access to Scotland's countryside. In August 1847 a party of naturalists, led by Professor John Hutton Balfour of the Royal Botanic Garden, attempted to walk through Glen Tilt by a horse road, which it believed was the public road between Braemar and Blair Atholl. They were met by the Duke of Atholl and some of his attendants. The Duke accused them of trespass, and tried to insist the party return by the road it had come, adding another twenty miles to their journey. They refused to do this, escaping over a wall beside the locked gate. The Duke took them to court but lost his case, establishing that the road was indeed a public right of way. The Duke was left to fume, literally, puffing on his clay pipe. This case led to the establishment of the principle of a reasonable freedom of movement in the hills, to a distinctive Scottish concept of trespass, and to the formation of the Scottish Rights of Way Society. The episode was recorded in verse by Douglas Maclagan, one of the party, and published as *The Battle o' Glen Tilt*.

from The Battle o' Glen Tilt

Some folk'll tak' a heap o' fash
For unco little end, man;
An' meikle time an' meikle cash
For nocht ava' they'll spend, man.
Thae chaps had come a hunder' miles
For what was hardly worth their while:
  'Twas a' to poo
  Some gerse that grew
  On Ben M'Dhu,
  That ne'er a coo
Would care to put her mouth till.

The Duke was at an unco loss
To manage in a hurry,
Sae he sent roun' the fiery cross,
To ca' the clan o' Murray.
His men cam' down frae glen an' hill-
Four gillies and a writer chiel-
  In kilts and hose,
  A' to oppose
  Their Saxon foes,
  An' gi'e them blows,
An' drive them frae the hills, man.

The Sassenachs they cam' doon to Blair,
And marched as bauld as brass, man;
The Glen was closed when they got there,
And out they could na' pass, man;
The Duke he glower'd in through the yett,
An' said that out they su'd na' get;

'Twas trespass clear
  Their comin' here,
  For they wad fear
  Awa' his deer,
Amang the Hielan' hills, man.

Balfour he said it was absurd;
The Duke was in a rage, man;
He said he wad na' hear a word,
Although they spak' an age, man.
The mair they fleeched, the mair they spoke,
The mair the Duke blew out his smoke.
  He said (guid lack!)
  Balfour micht tak'
  An' carry back
  His Saxon pack
Ayont the Hielan' hills, man.

The battle it was ended then,
Afore 'twas focht ava', man;
An' noo some ither chaps are gaen
To tak' the Duke to law, man.
Ochon! your Grace, my bonny man,
An' ye had sense as ye ha'e lan', man,
  Ye'd been this hour
  Ayont the po'er
  O' lawyers dour,
  An' let Balfour
Gang through your Hielan' hills, man.

Dougls Maclagan

What sort of plants should the walker look out for today in the Breadalbane hills? Surprisingly, in view of the problems they have to overcome, there is still a huge variety, albeit that the numbers of individual plants might be small in some areas. On the drive in to Inverlochlarig, Rob Roy's farmhouse, there's a meadow full of pink orchids in July. As you walk up from it to Beinn Tulaichean you pass the spikes of Bog Asphodel, topped with their yellow stars. I recall once taking the wrong path up Cruach Ardrain, and finding, in a boulder field just below the summit, three different species of saxifrage in flower, in a profusion not seen before or since. And what of the Lawers rarities?

Thank heavens, they're still there. The little pale blue Forget-Me-Not is shy, but worth looking for in sheltered spots. Purple Saxifrage grows on the ledges of vertical crags, flowering quite early in the season. It's where the Ben Lawers Schist outcrops high on the mountain that the characteristic plants show themselves. Alpine Lady's Mantle is common, even by the path. Also common are Moss Campion and Alpine Mouse-ear. Mountain Pansy has large purple flowers, and is found in the corries of the Ben. Scree slopes hold their own communities; in the wetter ones the Yellow Saxifrage, Mountain Sorrel and Alpine Pearlwort can be found. Dwarf willows creep over the rocks on the summit ridges, and on the south side of the mountain, if you are lucky, you may see the Mountain Gentian, an annual with flowers of a startling blue intensity.

Look by all means, but never pick – these plants are best left in their natural habitats. Take with you into the hills a little identification guide, and mark it as you find the plants – it's easier to replace than they are. Marvel also at the resonance of the plant names – Cyphel, Mountain Avens, Rose-root, Dwarf Cornel, Eyebright, Fleabane – they have their own poetry too.

Varieties of Blue.

Sky is one, sure;
an infinite kind,
deeper overhead
and paler at the edges -
or hadn't you noticed?
Look up, it's true.

Some bulbs flower in the year's opening -
Scilla, Iris, Glory-of-the-Snows.
Each one's a single blue word
on winter's blank sheet.

As the sun moves up
a new crop of hues
tries to catch our summer hopes.
Lithodora – 'Heavenly Blue';
Forget-me-not, a blended blue –
sky with some cloud stirred in.
Delphiniums stand up to be counted –
"I'm here", "And Me", "Me Too", "We're blue".

The blue beyond blue,
the truest, overwhelming Ace of Blue,
is Mountain Gentian.
Shyly, on mountain meadows,
it opens when the spring sun tells it,
ere evening azures into indigo.

Colin Will

from Mountains in Scotland
(3,000 Feet and Over)

from Tower Blocks in Glasgow
(Eight Floors and Over)

Neal Beggs

Ben Nevis 1344m - 4409ft ☐ Ben Macdui 1309m - 4295ft ☐ Braeriach 1296m - 4252ft ☐ Cairn Toul 1291m - 4236ft ☐ Sgor an Lochain Uaine - Cairn Toul 1258m - 4127ft ☐ Cairn Gorm 1244m - 4081ft ☐ Aonach Beag 1234m - 4049ft ☐ Aonach Mor 1221m - 4006ft ☐ Carn Mor Dearg 1220m - 4003ft ☐ Ben Lawers 1214m - 3983ft ☐ Beinn a'Bhuird - North Top 1197m - 3927ft ☐ Carn Eighe 1183m - 3881ft ☐ Beinn Mheadhoin 1182m - 3878ft ☐ Mam Sodhail 1181m - 3875ft ☐ Stob Choire Claurigh 1177m - 3862ft ☐ Ben More (Crianlarich) 1174m - 3852ft ☐ Ben Avon - Leabaidh an Daimh Bhuidhe 1171m - 3842ft ☐ Stob Binnein 1165m - 3822ft. ☐ Beinn Bhrotain 1157m - 3796ft ☐ Derry Cairngorm 1155m - 3789ft ☐ Lochnagar - Cac carn Beag 1155m - 3789ft ☐ Sgurr nan Ceathreamhnan 1151m - 3776ft ☐ Bidean nam Bian 1150m - 3773ft ☐ Sgurr na Lapaich 1150m - 3773ft ☐ Ben Alder 1148m - 3766ft ☐ Geal-Charn 1132m - 3714ft ☐ Binnein Mor 1130m - 3707ft ☐ Ben Lui 1130m - 3707ft ☐ An Riabhachan 1129m - 3704ft ☐ Creag Meagaidh 1128m - 3701ft ☐ Ben Cruachan 1126m - 3694ft ☐ Carn nan Gabhar 1121m - 3678ft o A'Chralaig 1120m - 3674ft o An Stuc 1118m - 3668ft ☐ Meall Garbh 1118m - 3668ft ☐ Sgor Gaoith 1118m - 3668ft ☐ Aonach Beag (Alder District) 1116m - 3661ft ☐ Stob Coire an laoigh 1116m - 3661ft ☐ Stob Coire Easain 1115m - 3658ft ☐ Monadh Mor 1113m - 3652ft ☐ Tom a'Choinich 1112m - 3648ft ☐ Carn a'Choire Bhoidheach 1110m - 3642ft ☐ Sgurr Mor 1110m - 3642ft ☐ Sgurr nan Conbhairean 1109m - 3638ft ☐ Meall a'Bhuiridh 1108m - 3635ft ☐ Stob a'Choire Mheadhoin 1105m - 3625ft ☐ Beinn Ghlas 1103m - 3619ft ☐ Beinn Eibhinn 1102m - 3615ft ☐ Mullach Fraoch-choire 1102m - 3615ft ☐ Creise 1100m - 3609ft ☐ Sgurr a'Mhaim 1099m - 3606ft ☐ Sgurr Choinnich Mor 1094m - 3589ft ☐ Sgurr nan Clach Geala 1093m - 3586ft ☐ Bynack More 1090m - 3576ft ☐ Stob Ghabhar 1090m - 3576ft ☐ Beinn a'Chlachair 1087m - 3566ft ☐ Beinn Dearg 1084m - 3556ft ☐ Beinn a'Chaorainn 1083m - 3553ft ☐ Schiehallion 1083m - 3553ft ☐ Sgurr a'Choire Ghlais 1083m - 3553ft ☐ Beinn a'Chreachain 1081m - 3547ft ☐ Beinn Heasgarnich 1078m - 3537ft ☐ Ben Starav 1078m - 3537ft ☐ Beinn Dorain 1076m - 3530ft ☐ Stob Coire Sgreamhach 1072m - 3517ft ☐ Braigh Coire Chruinn-bhalgain 1070m - 3510ft ☐ An Socach 1069m - 3507ft ☐ Meall Corranaich 1069m - 3507ft ☐ Glas Maol 1068m - 3504ft ☐ Sgurr Fhuaran 1067m - 3501ft ☐ Cairn of Claise 1064m - 3491ft ☐ Bidein a'Ghlas Thuill - An Teallach 1062m - 3484ft ☐ Sgurr Fiona - An Teallach 1060m - 3478ft ☐ Na Gruagaichean 1056m - 3465ft ☐ Spidean a'Choire Leith - Liathach 1055m - 3461ft ☐ Stob Poite Coire Ardair 1054m - 3458ft ☐ Toll Creagach 1054m - 3458ft ☐ Sgurr a'Chaorachain 1053m - 3455ft ☐ Glas Tulaichean 1051m - 3448ft ☐ Beinn a'Chaorainn 1049m - 3442ft ☐ Geal Charn - Mullach Coire an Iubhair 1049m - 3442ft ☐ Sgurr Fhuar-thuill 1049m - 3442ft ☐ Carn an t-Sagairt Mor 1047m - 3435ft ☐ Creag Mhor 1047m - 3435ft ☐ Glas Leathad Mor - Ben Wyvis 1046m - 3432ft ☐ Chno Dearg 1046m - 3432ft ☐ Cruach Ardrain 1046m - 3432ft ☐ Beinn Iutharn Mhor 1045m - 3428ft ☐ Meall nan Tarmachan 1044m - 3425ft ☐ Stob Coir'an Albannaich 1044m - 3425ft ☐ Carn Mairg 1041m - 3415ft ☐ Sgurr na Ciche 1040m - 3412ft o Meall Ghaordie 1039m - 3409ft ☐ Beinn Achaladair 1038m - 3406ft o Carn a'Mhaim 1037m - 3402ft o Sgurr a'Bhealaich Dheirg 1036m - 3399ft ☐ Gleouraich 1035m - 3396ft ☐ Carn Dearg 1034m - 3392ft ☐ Am Bodach 1032m - 3386ft ☐ Beinn Fhada (Ben Attow) 1032m - 3386ft ☐ Ben Oss 1029m - 3376ft ☐ Carn an Righ 1029m - 3376ft ☐ Carn Gorm 1029m - 3376ft ☐ Sgurr a'Mhaoraich 1027m - 3369ft ☐ Sgurr na Ciste Duibhe 1027m - 3369ft ☐ Ben Challum 1025m - 3363ft ☐ Sgorr Dhearg - Beinn a'Bheithir 1024m - 3360ft ☐ Mullach an Rathain - Liathach 1023m - 3356ft ☐ Aonach air Chrith 1021m - 3350ft ☐ Stob Dearg - Buachaille Etive More 1021m - 3350ft ☐ Ladhar Bheinn 1020m - 3346ft ☐ Beinn Bheoil

11 Mitchellhill Rd 196m. - 643ft. □ 9 Mitchellhill Rd 193.5m - 635ft □ 7 Mitchellhill Rd 190.5m - 625ft □ 5 Mitchellhill Rd 187.4m - 615ft □ 3 Mitchellhill Rd 183.8m - 603ft □ 198 Balgrayhill Rd 175.3m - 575ft □ 178 Balgrayhill Rd 175.1m - 574ft □ 21 Birnie Court 171.6m - 563ft □ 42 Viewpiont Plc 169.9m - 557ft □ 22 Viewpiont Plc 169.9m - 557ft □ Waterbank Heights, 25 Dougrie Pl 169.9m - 557ft □ Muirhouse Heights, 21 Dougrie Pl 165.2m - 542ft □ Kittoch Heights, 33 Dougrie Pl 165.2m - 542ft □ 10 Red Road Court 163.4m - 536ft □ 123 Petershill Drive 160m - 525ft □ 93 Petershill Drive 158m - 518ft □ 33 Petershill Court, David Naismith Court, Apart-Hotel, YMCA, 157.9m - 518ft □ 63 Petershill Drive 157m - 515ft □ 213 - 183 - 153 Petershill Drive 153m - 502ft □ 10 - 20 - 30 Petershill Cresent 150m - 492ft □ 250 Edgefauld Rd 150m - 492ft □ 20 Rosemount St 144.5m - 474ft □ 15 Croftbank St 143.8m - 472ft □ 40 Rosemount St 143.m - 469ft □ 25 Soutra Place 133.m - 436ft □ 15 Forge Plc 130.8m - 429ft □ 15 Coll Plc 130.5m - 428ft □ 29 Glenavon Rd 127.6m - 419ft □ 7 Longstone Place 127m - 417ft □ 71 Glenavon Rd 126.7m - 416ft □ 115 Glenavon Rd 124.3m - 408ft □ 6 - 8 Fountainwell Square 122.2m - 401ft □ 80 Charles St 120.8m - 396ft □ Lomond House 140 Charles St 120.5m - 395ft □ 17 - 19 Pinkston Drive 120.2m - 394ft □ 90 Charles St 120.1m - 394ft □ 32 - 34 Pinkston Drive 120.1m - 394ft □ 2 - 4 Fountainwell Terrace 119.5m - 392ft □ 138 Fastnet St 119m - 390ft □ 2 Taylor Place 118.9m - 390ft □ Westercommon 109 Wester Common Rd 118.6m - 389ft □ 15 Grafton Plc 118.6m - 389ft □ 16- 18 Pinkston Drive 118.5m - 389ft □ Crawfurd Heights 31 - 35 Pinkston Drive 118.4m - 388ft □ Saracen 151 Wester Common Rd 118.3m - 388ft □ 3 - 5 Pinkston Drive 118.2m - 388ft □ Nevis House 150 Charles St 117m - 384ft □ Tennant Heights 37 - 49 Fountainwell Avenue 116.4m - 382ft □ Possil 231 Wester Common Rd 115.8m - 380ft □ Campsie House 160 Charles St 115.8m - 380ft □ 53 Carbisdale St 115.1m - 378ft □ 109 Whitevale St 115.1m - 378ft □ Gowrie 120 Wyndford Rd 114.9m - 377ft □ 51 Whitevale St 114.8m - 377ft □ Keppoch 187 Wester Common Rd 114.5m - 376ft □ 39 Linkwood Crescent 113m - 371ft □ 76 Collina St 113m - 371ft □ 7 St Mungo Plc 112.2m - 368ft □ 15 Eccles St 112m - 367ft □ 12 Dobbies Loan Plc 111.9m - 367ft □ 15 Scaraway Drive 111.8m - 367ft □ 61 Scaraway Drive 111.7m - 366ft □ 12 Eccles St 111m - 364ft □ Barony Heights 14 - 18 Fountainwell Plc 110.9m - 364ft □ Blaker 191 Wyndford Rd 109.8m - 360ft □ Rodgers 171 Wyndford Rd 109.1m - 358ft □ 27 Linkwood Crescent 109m - 358ft □ Eagle Heights 2 - 4 Fountainwell Plc 108.8m - 357ft □ 195 Fernbank St 108.5m - 356ft □ Edwards 151 Wyndford Rd 108.3m - 355ft □ 62 Strowan St 107.7m - 353ft □ 30 Balbeggie St 106.8m - 350ft □ 135 Scaraway Drive 107.3m - 352ft □ 123Castlebay Drive 106.5m - 349ft □ 69 Castlebay Drive 106.3m - 349ft □ 145 Shawhill Rd 105m - 344ft □ 27 Castlebay Drive 104.6m - 343ft □ 15 Linkwood Crescent 104m - 341ft □ Lorne Court 9 Cedar Court 103.3m - 339ft □ 60 Strowan St 102.4m - 336ft □ 22 Dundasvale Court 102m - 335ft □ 20 Balbeggie St 102m - 335ft □ 2 Dundasvale Court 101.8m - 334ft □ 6 Dundasvale Court 101.8m - 334ft □ Katrine Court 65 Cedar St 101.8m - 334ft □ Torridon Court 104 Cedar St 100.6m - 330ft □ 39 Rosemount St 100m - 328ft □ 32 Fearnmore Rd 99.2m - 325ft □ 4 Fearnmore Rd 99.1m - 325ft □ 60 Fearnmore Rd 98.9m - 324ft □ 88 Fearnmore Rd 98.6m - 323ft □ 120 Fearnmore Rd 96.5m - 316.6ft □ Flemington 70 Kennishead Ave 94m - 308ft □ Woodfoot 60 Kennishead Ave 93.5m - 307ft □ Melford 50 Kennishead Ave 93m - 305ft □ 31 Birness Drive 92.5m - 303ft □ Williamwood 40 Kennishead Ave 92.5m - 303ft □ Anniesland Court, 843 Gt. Western Rd 92m - 302ft □ Alderwood, 30 Kennishead Ave 92m - 302ft □ Mcgill, 124 Shawbridge St 91.6m - 301ft □ Campbell, 12 Riverford Road 91.3m - 300ft □ Woodrow, 142 Shawbridge

The Material World Shifting Through Us

Gerrie Fellows & Tom Prentice

The Material World Shifting Through Us

This is not about geography but time.

It was always about time.

Crampons scratching over timespans of frozen water, heather, rock.

And time was never our strong point.

Why we picked Rev. Ted's Gully I don't know, but the weather and conditions weren't great so I wouldn't have wanted to go too far into the coire. The higher we went, the more snow and the longer and more complicated the descent. The climb goes at a reasonable grade and I have a strong recollection of there already being people on the route. And once we were at the top we'd be on a broad ridge; it'd be just a matter of following Gearr Aonach to the end and descending the Zig-Zags. I'd taken that way off before.

I don't really remember the route until the last section, the top hundred metres or so, probably because up to that point there was a reasonable amount of snow and ice and the climbing was straightforward. I have a recollection that the conditions were typical Glen Coe; patches of ice and good snow mixed in with softer and less consolidated stuff; with lots of small rowans and heather poking out.

By the time I was on the final pitches the wind had got up and there was a fair amount of snow lashing about; new, soft snow mixed with old, sharp spindrift. It wasn't desperate, but I remember an urgency to get to the top and get off before things got worse. This was complicated by the terrain. The climb had steepened and it became clear it was going to be harder than expected. Everything was covered with a crust of white powder too superficial to support any weight. I remember moving out of the gully on to the semi-vertical heather of the left-hand wall.

A moment. High up on the route, the gully thinned out. He leads into thin unconsolidated powder, spiky grass. It has begun to snow. He's taking a long time on the pitch; suddenly the pace of the route has changed, the urgency of the day. It's snowing hard now. The route thinnned out to almost nothing. Time. Light beginning to go or maybe she just thinks about time, poised there at the stance, watching, feeding the frozen belay ropes through mittened hands. Cold now, the spindrift finding its way under her collar, sifting down her neck.

I distinctly remember running it out on this semi-vertical heather without any or much protection, despite trying to place things here and there. I remember controlling a growing state of anxiety, aware that making this sort of climbing safe is time-consuming, but the day was moving on and time wasn't something we had a lot of.

At the top of the route, blizzard. Windroar. Spikes of snowy light.

A lot of wind and snow flying about; visibility was limited, but reasonable enough. It was still day, but the remaining light was going fast. I think it was snowing.

She doesn't know which way the wind comes from. It comes from everywhere, is all around them; they are immersed in it, wrapped round by it. It roars in their ears.

There were footsteps still from the party ahead, leading off down Gearr Aonach to the Zig-Zags, and having packed the gear away – the ropes would have been stiff and snow-covered – and got out compasses and map we set off north-east into the wind.

She's aware of trying to keep her mind working without its usual reference points, senses engulfed. They have the compasses out, taking a bearing, the needle quivers and jigs over the buckling map, the wind yanks at it, would swirl it away, buffets their crouched backs, their swaddled, helmeted faces. They stand up into it again and she sees him turn 180 degrees, as if setting off away from the bearing. The wind tugs and pulls at him, wild dancing. No, she yells out, touches his arm.

I began to doubt my decision. In a snowstorm at night there was a chance we'd miss the top of the Zig-Zags. I knew the descent, but not well and mostly in the other world of summer. Surrounded by steep ground with no other way down we'd be forced to back-track anyway.

But where were we? At the top of the route or further along the ridge to the north-east, about to turn on a walk I don't remember taking, a blank of swirling snow into which our younger selves have disappeared?

We turned about, heading south-west along Gearr Aonach to a point from where we could contour easy-angled slopes into the head of the Lost Valley and make our descent.

The front of her crampon, one of those old hinged ones, kicks loose from her boot. She stops and takes it off, wedges the boot back in, pulls the straps tight. Five minutes later it happens again. Snow packs into the space between crampon and boot. They tighten and re-tighten the straps, both of them. She will remember this, a refrain on the descent, taking off stiff, frozen layers of overmitt, working with numb fingers against the prickling metal. And somewhere in the deep snow, her crampon slipping off every two steps, unable to make progress, she will give up on it. Will go half lame, ice-axe poised to break a slide.

I remember it snowing, but once off the ridge the wind dropped away. *Yes, a stillness.* These southern slopes are classic places for snow deposition and therefore windslab build-up. I hadn't thought about that at the time, but I remember being very concerned about the state of the snow.

He crosses the slope first and she watches him safe across, as intently as later she'll watch him prusiking up a jammed rope on Hoy, the wind billowing the rope and his body out over the waves, and will think, I don't want ever to have to do this. But now, at the beginning of things, in the first seasons of love, she starts across herself, wading into the deep snow, gains a rocky spur, the far shore.

There must still have been some light: my memories are of large open slopes of new snow, stillness and brightness. The sky was white and the snow reflected this. I remember the descent as being quite intense: I was relieved to reach the valley floor.

His headtorch battery's going now, a faint wash of yellow light. Neither of them has a spare. But by this time they're down into the valley. And it keeps him with her; for once he isn't moving too fast. Lame and blind, they keep together.

The rest of the descent I don't really remember; it was probably dark and the lack of a headtorch would have been a drag. I think we got a bit lost at the boulder choke – through lack of light and the snow.

The lost valley is warm. The rowans of the valley mouth, sweet shelter. They stop to drink the last lukewarm coffee, Allt Coire Gabhail somewhere under ice and boulders.

They cross the bridge and go up past the Meeting of Three Waters, put their shoulders to the door of the doss and push into yellow gaslight, steam of food, wet clothes and talk. Ronnie and Roger, go-for-it lads, have come off the Zig-Zags.

Someone we didn't know benighted up there that night.

Beside the Alt-na-reigh the doss turns back to rust and earth.

It must be sixteen years since we set out on that route.

Move by move passing through time.

A narrative.

Yet all I have in my hands is a fragment. All I know of the ascent now is a moment of knowledge: the easy route suddenly serious, snow turning to blizzard.

The moment in which we find ourselves in a country with different rules of survival.

The border shifting, elusive, unknown until we have crossed it.

It has to do with time and weather; cloud level, altitude, the transformation of water to ice, ice to water.

It's the point where the material world; its crystals of snow and rhyolite, the gnarled branches of heather, shifts through us.

It isn't purely to do with risk, though that alertness is there too.

The sense of having to make your way out of a landscape in which we do not exist.

Perhaps we're always more conscious of this in descent, emerging out of danger; in darkness crossing the snowline or walking on a bearing out of mist.

But that other country is always there; it lay in wait for us that morning, curled in the weather forecast like a cat; it's here as you leave for the Alps. It lies in wait over the summer hills, over the hazy August ridge of Gearr Aonach. It shifts through us as we walk for we are transparent creatures made of molecules.

Monsieur the Acrobat!

I crossed the Channel on the 29th of July 1863, embarrassed by the possession of two ladders, each twelve feet long, which joined together like those used by firemen, and shut up like parallel rulers. My luggage was highly suggestive of housebreaking, for, besides these, there were several coils of rope, and numerous tools of suspicious appearance, and it was reluctantly admitted into France, but it passed through the customhouse with less trouble than I anticipated, after a timely expenditure of a few francs.

I am not in love with the douane. It is the purgatory of travellers, where uncongenial spirits mingle together for a time, before they are separated into rich and poor. The douaniers look upon tourists as their natural enemies; see how eagerly they pounce upon the portmanteaux! One of them has discovered something! He has never seen its like before, and he holds it aloft in the face of its owner, with inquisitorial insolence. "But *what* is this?" The explanation is only half-satisfactory. "But what is *this*?" says he, laying hold of a little box. "Powder." "But that it is forbidden to carry of powder on the railway." "Bah!" says another and older hand, "pass the effects of Monsieur"; and our countryman – whose cheeks had begun to redden under the stares of his fellow-travellers – is allowed to depart with his half-worn tooth-brush, while the discomfited douanier gives a mighty shrug at the strange habits of those "whose insular position excludes them from the march of continental ideas."

My real troubles commenced at Susa. The officials there, more honest and more obtuse than the Frenchmen, declined at one and the same time to be bribed, or to pass my baggage until a satisfactory account of it was rendered; and, as they refused to believe the true explanation, I was puzzled by what to say, but was presently relieved from the dilemma by one of the men, who was cleverer than his fellows, suggesting that I was going to Turin to exhibit in the streets; that I mounted the ladder and balanced myself on the end of it, then lighted my pipe and put the point of the bâton in its bowl, and caused the bâton to gyrate around my head. The rope was to keep back the spectators, and an Englishman in my company was the agent. "Monsieur is acrobat then?" "Yes, certainly." "Pass the effects of Monsieur the acrobat!"

Edward Whymper, from *Scrambles Amongst the Alps*, 1871

Vertigo

Then they came to the very edge of the cliff and looked down.
Below, a real world flowed in its parts, green, green.
The two elements touched – rock, air.
She thought of where the mind opened out
into the sheer drop of its intelligence,
the updrafting pastures of the vertical in which a bird now rose,
blue body the blue wind was knifing upward
faster than it could naturally rise,
up into the downdraft until it was frozen until she could see them at last.
The stages of flight, broken down, broken free,
each wingflap folding, each splay of the feather-sets flattening
for entry. . . . *Parts* she thought, *free* parts, watching the laws
at work, *through which desire must course*
seeking an ending, seeking a shape. Until the laws of flight and fall
   increased.
Until they made, all of an instant, a bird, a blue
enchantment of properties no longer
knowable. What is it to understand, she let fly,
leaning outward from the edge now that the others had gone down.
How close can the two worlds get, the movement from one to the other
being death? She tried to remember from the other life
the passage of the rising notes off the violin
into the air, thin air, chopping their way in,
wanting to live forever – marrying, marrying – yet still free of the
   orchestral swelling

which would at any moment pick them up, in-
corporate. How is it one soul wants to be owned
by a single other
in its entirety? –
What is it sucks one down, offering itself, only itself, for
ever? She saw the cattle below
moving in a shape which was exactly their hunger.
She saw – could they be men? – the plot. She leaned. How does one enter
a story? Where the cliff and air pressed the end of each other,
everything else in the world – woods, fields, stream, start of another darker
woods – appeared as kinds of
falling. She listened for the wind again. What was it in there she could hear
that has nothing to do with *telling the truth?*
What was it that was *not her listening?*
She leaned out. What is it pulls at one, she wondered,
what? That it has no shape but point of view?
That it cannot move to hold us?
Oh it has vibrancy, she thought, this emptiness, this intake just prior to
the start of a story, the mind trying to fasten
and fasten, the mind feeling it like a sickness this wanting
to snag, catch hold, begin, the mind crawling out to the edge of the cliff
and feeling the body as if for the first time – how it cannot
follow, cannot love.

Jorie Graham

I Shut My Hands

One has a pair of hands and they obey. How are one's orders transmitted to one's hands?

I had made a discovery which horrified me: my hands were numb. My hands were dead. They sent me no message. Probably they had been numb a long time and I had not noticed it. The pity was that I had noticed it, had raised the question. That was serious.

Lashed by the wind, the wings of the plane had been dragging and jerking at the cables by which they were controlled from the stick, and the stick in my hands had not ceased jerking a single second. I had been gripping the stick with all my might for forty minutes, fearful lest the strain snap the cables. So desperate had been my grip that now I could not feel my hands.

What a discovery! My hands were not my own. I looked at them and decided to lift a finger: it obeyed me. I looked away and issued the same order: now I could not feel whether the finger had obeyed or not. No message had reached me. I thought: 'Suppose my hands were to open: how would I know it?' I swung my head round and looked again: my hands were still locked round the wheel. Nevertheless, I was afraid. How can a man tell the difference between the sight of a hand opening and the decision to open that hand, when there is no longer an exchange of sensations between the hand and the brain? How can one tell the difference between an image and an act of the will? Better stop thinking of the picture of open hands. Hands live a life of their own. Better not offer them this monstrous temptation. And I began to chant a silly litany which went on uninterruptedly until this flight was over. A single thought. A single image. A single phrase tirelessly chanted over and over again: 'I shut my hands. I shut my hands. I shut my hands.' All of me was condensed into that phrase and for me the white sea, the whirling eddies, the saw-toothed range ceased to exist. There was only 'I shut my hands.'

There was no danger, no cyclone, no land unattained. Somewhere there was a pair of rubber hands which, once they let go the wheel, could not possibly come alive in time to recover from the tumbling drop into the sea.

Antoine de Saint-Exupery, from *Wind, Sand and Stars,* 1939
translated by Lewis Galantière

Report to Someone

We think we're all there is, then the big light,
and a call comes and everyone understands.
All right, we're lonely: trees never need us, and
wind in its wandering visits us then goes away.
And we can't see it but we think there's a light inside
everything. Even at night it wants out and pushes
quietly, insistently on the wall with its tiny hands.

In the silence that comes flooding down from the mountains
a shapeless lament begins to press toward sound.
It can wait: it gains by every day
of being unrecognised. Without moving
it explores a way to be ready, and when
pieces of time break off it follows them,
alive in their being and unknown but true.

William Stafford

Tasting Bear Meat

"Let's go, shall we?" he said to me one day in February – which in his language meant that, since the weather was good, we should leave in the afternoon for the winter climb of the Tooth of M., which for some weeks had been one of our projects. We slept in an inn and left the next day, not too early, at some undetermined hour (Sandro did not like watches: he felt their quiet continuous admonishment to be an arbitrary intrusion). We plunged boldly into the fog and came out of it about one o'clock, in gleaming sunlight and on the big crest of a peak which was not the right one.

I then said that we should be able to go down about a hundred metres, cross over halfway up the mountain, and go up along the next ridge: or, better yet, since we were already there, continue climbing and be satisfied with the wrong peak, which in any case was only forty metres lower than the right one. But Sandro, with splendid bad faith, said in a few dense syllables that my last proposal was fine, but from there "by way of the easy northwest ridge" (this was a sarcastic quotation from the abovementioned Alpine Club guide) we could also reach the Tooth of M. in half an hour; and what was the point of being twenty if you couldn't permit yourself the luxury of taking the wrong route.

The easy ridge must really have been easy, indeed elementary in the summer; but we found it in a very discomforting state. The rock was wet on the side facing the sun and covered with a black layer of ice in the shade; between one large outcrop of rock and another lay pockets of melting snow into which we sank to our waists. We reached the top at five; I dragged myself along so pitifully that it was painful, while Sandro was seized by a sinister hilarity that I found very annoying.

"And how do we get down?"

"As for getting down, we shall see," he replied, and added mysteriously: "The worst that can happen is to have to taste bear meat."

Well, we tasted bear meat in the course of that night, which seemed very, very long. We got down in two hours, helped badly by the rope, which was frozen; it had become a malignant, rigid tangle that snagged on each projection and rang against the rock face like the cable of a funicular. At seven we were on the bank of a frozen pond and it was dark. We ate the little that was left, built a useless dry stone wall facing the wind, and lay down on the ground to sleep, pressed to each other. It was as though time itself had frozen; every so often we got to our feet to reactivate our circulation, and it was always the same time: the wind never stopped blowing, there was always the same ghost of a moon, always at the same point in the sky, and in front of the moon passed a fantastic cavalcade of tattered clouds, always the same. We had taken off our shoes, as described in Lammer's books, so dear to Sandro, and we kept our feet in our packs; at the first funereal light, which seemed to seep from the snow and not the sky, we rose with our limbs benumbed and our eyes glittering from lack of sleep, hunger and the hardness of our bed. And we found our shoes so frozen that they rang like bells, and to get them on we had to hatch them out like brood hens.

But we went back down to the valley under our own steam; and to the innkeeper who asked us, with a snicker, how things had gone, and meanwhile was staring at our wild, exalted faces, we answered flippantly that we had had an excellent outing, then paid the bill and departed with dignity. This was it – the bear meat; and now that many years have passed, I regret that I ate so little of it, for nothing has had, even distantly, the taste of that meat, which is the taste of being strong and free, free also to make mistakes and be the master of one's destiny. That is why I am grateful to Sandro for having led me consciously into trouble, on that trip and other undertakings which were only apparently foolish, and I am certain that they helped me later on.

They didn't help Sandro, or not for long. Sandro was Sandro Delmastro, the first man to be killed fighting in the Resistance with the Action Party's Piedmontese Military Command. After a few months of extreme tension, in April of 1944 he was captured by the Fascists, did not surrender and tried to escape from the Fascist Party house in Cuneo. He was killed with a tommygun burst in the back of the neck by a monstrous child-executioner, one of those wretched murderers of fifteen whom Mussolini's Republic of Salò recruited in the reformatories. His body was abandoned in the road for a long time because the Fascists had forbidden the population to bury him.

Today I know that it is a hopeless task to try to dress a man in words, make him live again on the printed page, especially a man like Sandro. He was not the sort of person you can tell stories about, nor to whom one erects monuments – he who laughed at all monuments: he lived completely in his deeds, and when they were over nothing of him remains – nothing but words, precisely.

Primo Levi, from *The Periodic Table*, 1975
translated by Raymond Rosenthal

By the Loch of the Green Corrie

Andrew Greig

A Quest

It was the last time I saw Norman MacCaig, some time after midnight in his flat with the Glenmorangie near empty. We'd been talking about fishing and the Highlands, all those places he could never go again. Around us were so many books and photos, mementos of a life.

On impulse I asked "What is your favourite place in the world?" A long pause. That great head swivelled my way. "Assynt." "Yes I know it's Assnyt," I said. "But where?" A longer pause. My eyes drifted to the mantelpiece and pictures of MacDiarmid, Norman's great friend A. K. McLeod, and a photo of four beaming honoured men: MacCaig, Sorley McLean, Iain Crichton Smith and Seamus Heaney. I'd always loved that photo for its comradeship, the warmth and respect among such completely different artistic spirits.

"The Loch of the Green Corrie," Norman said at last. Pause. "But it's not called that." Pause. "But if you go to Lochinver and ask for a man named Norman MacAskill, *if* he likes you he may tell where it is. I should like you to fish there for me. If you catch a fish I shall be delighted. If you don't …" Pause. Poets like comedians must have the gift of timing. "… I shall be most amused, looking down from a place I don't believe in." Shortly after, we said goodnight. My father's last words to me had been "Thanks for coming to see me." Norman's were simply "Ta-ta." Typical concision, thanks you and goodnight in one. But a charge had been laid on me, a quest, a homage.

So Many Summers

Beside one loch, a hind's neat skeleton,
Beside another, a boat pulled high and dry:
Two neat geometries drawn in the weather:
Two things already dead and still to die.

I passed them every summer, rod in hand,
Skirting the bright blue or the spitting gray,
And, every summer, saw how the bleached timbers
Gaped wider and the neat ribs fell away.

Time adds one malice to another one –
Now you'd look very close before you knew
If it's the boat that ran, the hind went sailing.
So many summers, and I have lived them too.

Of all the hills in Scotland, the Assynt ones are the strangest and closest to my heart. There may be no ruined stones, but there certainly are ruined mountains. Cul Mor, Cul Beag, Stac Polly, Canisp, Ben Mor Assynt, Suilven – they rise, each separate in its terrible grand isolation, from a dark, lochan-sprinkled moor. Each worn down, utterly distinct as Norman's photo of the four grand old men, disintegrated, beautiful. Three years after MacCaig's death I at last drove with my fishing partners the Dorward brothers past Inchnadamph and Loch Assynt and sprawled Quinag like a slumped tent of stone. It was a bright July afternoon. The car was loaded with tents, packs, food and fishing gear. We were ready.

I parked in Lochinver, next to the surgery where my father used to do locums after he retired, the origin of my bond to Assynt. I was heading for Tourist Information when I saw a butcher shop: A. MacAskill. I went in, asked if they knew where Norman lived. Of course. The young woman pointed it out. "I think he's in."

I rang the bell. Waited. I was nervous. MacCaig's "*If* he likes you" was in my head. Eventually he came to the door, a large, elderly, silent man who looked me over. "Yes?" "I'm Andrew Greig," I said, "I'm here about Norman MacCaig." A long silence, a long look. "You'd better come in."

We sat in the sitting room and looked at each other. I explained my quest for the Loch of the Green Corrie, the charge MacCaig had laid on me, how I needed to know its real name and whereabouts. I didn't add the "*If* he likes you." Norman MacAskill is a man of few words and long silences and slight deafness. Put together with my anxiety, it was rather intimidating. I resolved to try not to gabble like an over-eager townie journalist come to rip off Norman's memory.

When I'd finished, we looked at each other. A long silence. "And did you know Norman well?" I tried to say Yes and No. I'd known him over thirty years but of course he was a very private man for all his sociability, and I wouldn't claim to know him that well but he'd refereed applications for me and we met at readings and in the last years of his life I often visited the flat . . . I was gabbling. I stopped. We sat and looked at each other.

"Norman fished a lot of lochs in Assynt. In fact, probably more than anyone else. The Loch of the Green Corrie . . ." Pause. Come on, come on. Give me it. "We used to go there with A. K. McLeod." "I know," I said, "he told me. He loved the place."

Long pause. A very long pause. I was resolved to keep my mouth shut. Eventually Norman MacAskill looked directly at me. "I miss him," he said simply. "I know," I said. "I miss him too." And we sat there.

At length he took a pencil from his breast pocket. I opened my map. The pencil hovered. He put on his glasses and looked again. Come on, come on! Then, beautiful!, the pencil descended, X marks the spot. "Here." Yes! "It's a steep climb. And if the wind's from the East it's no use. We used big flies, size 10 to 12, mostly Black Pennel and Zulus." I scarcely heard him, my head still spinning with relief as I left.

A loch in the moors off the Kylesku road. We stumbled over burns, heather and peat hags and set up camp there. A little Glenlivet, tasting as always so much sweeter outdoors. Then a spot of evening fishing. Five trout, all small, but it wasn't the Loch of the Green Corrie so it didn't count. I fell asleep with the tent fabric rapping above my head, thinking of the Himalayas, thinking of MacCaig and scraps of his poems that seem pasted to this wild, ruinous country.

Next morning. A steep climb and no mistake. No wonder MacCaig had had to stop going there. The wonder is he found it at all. Up steep gullies and ramps, rough and boulder-strewn. Sweating with our lunch and fishing gear in our day-packs. Thinking of the trio of the two Normans and A. K. coming this same way with high hearts thirty years ago. Past one loch system. Up a gully and into another. Up past that and after two hours we arrived.

It's a gem all right. Yes, green rough grass and screeds of grey scree. Held in a bowl, secluded, quiet, its own world. Quinag in the distance. Nothing else. We fitted up our rods and got started. The wind, of course, was brisk and from the East, and at 2,000 feet it was chill when the sun went in.

Peter Dorward got a nibble five minutes in but lost it. He shrugged and sent out his line again with one simple flick. He'd been taught by his father, has a lovely cast. From Strathkiness, he's now a doctor in London. He's also a writer – his brilliant story about the dissolute latter days of Oor Wullie and his gang raised quite a stushie and had to be withdrawn under legal threats from D.C.Thompson. His brother Andrew had been heavily involved in the Poetry Society and Polygon at Edinburgh University and he was now running bol.com in New York. Very twenty-first century, how different from MacCaig's friends and time. And yet here we are, fishing in their name at their loch, and our sense of loyalty and belonging goes deep.

We fish, we break, we fish again. Hours pass as we cover the loch. A couple of early rises, then nothing. "Wind from the East - no use."

It's cold when the mist comes in, when clouds roll down the corrie. Sounds of water, wind over grass, occasional shrill keek of a lone bird of prey. The Loch of the Green Corrie begins to sink into me. The slope opposite rises like a breaking frozen wave of grey and green. I picture two Normans and A. K. fishing right here on good days and bad. MacAskill said MacCaig was hilariously and endlessly inventive with his name-calling when one of them failed to hold a fish.

"If you don't enjoy fishing even when you don't catch a fish, you shouldn't be a fisherman," Peter says as we pack up our gear. Right enough, for all that we failed to catch anything, it's been a rich day. I remember telling MacCaig about a year before he died that I first resolved to be a published poet when I read four of his Assynt poems in the *Weekend Scotsman* in about 1968. One of them, 'Rich Day', I'd never forgotten. "Oh yes," MacCaig said quizzically, "and how does that one go?" Great bullshit detector. Luckily I was still able to recite it in full to him there in the Auld Toll Bar in Bruntsfield:

Rich Day

All day we fished
the loch clasped in the throat
of Canisp that scrawny mountain,
and caught trout and
invisible treasures.

We walked home, ragged millionaires,
our minds jingling, our fingers
rustling the air.

And now, lying on the warm sand,
we see
the rim of the full moon
rest on a formal corrugation of water
at the feet of
a Britannia cloud:
sea and sky, one golden sovereign
that will never be spent.

Norman peered at me. I swear he was moved. He'd heard one of his poems recited across thirty years. He picked up his whisky. "That's quite good," he said. Drank. "I quite like that." Bizarrely it doesn't seem to be in any of his *Collected Poems*.

We pack up and head on down the rough slopes. As we brew up by our tents we talk about the day and decide to go back again tomorrow. The wind might have changed. We owe the past another day.

After eating and Glenlivet, talk turns to death (we're in our mid-life, when the brevity of it all starts to sink in). Peter says he absolutely doesn't believe in any afterlife. But some of him will remain in the people he has affected, met, spoken with, loved. His wife and children and friends. "That's immortality enough," he concludes. "That's worth trying to be a good person for." We sip whisky and look over our darkening loch, and I think how MacCaig, who didn't believe in an afterlife either, would recognize and embrace that outlook. And how he does indeed live on, in the Loch of the Green Corrie, in every head that carries a memory of him or scrap of his poetry. That'll have to do.

Next day we sweated back up to the loch again, wind still from the East and North. On the way, many tiny frogs bouncing around in the coarse grass. Last reading I heard MacCaig give, sitting down, finally old and frail, he said "When I am dead – which will be quite soon – I shall probably be known as the frog poet. They say I write a lot of poems about frogs. I do. I like them. This is a poem about a frog . . ." I bend down and scoop one in my palm. Look at it hard, the pulse in its throat. It leaps from my hand and is gone, and it has gladdened my heart.

We set up rods and fish all day in that ruined landscape. Much like yesterday, cloud and sun and wind. At least the chill wind keeps the midgies as well as the fish at bay. I'm thinking a lot about Norman, remembering his mischief and his generosity. His delight in company and his privacy. His humility and his pride. His avowed distrust of philosophy and his metaphysical instincts. His friendship with Chris Grieve who as Hugh MacDiarmid often had so many qualities MacCaig detested – bombast, self-importance, badly-digested philosophy, combative aggression, incomprehensibility. Maybe we can all be presented as contrary and contradictory, but Norman MacCaig was more than most.

So the day goes on. We cast, retrieve, cast. At least I'm getting better at this, my line not tangling or catching on me or the bank despite the gusting wind. When my friend Mal Duff died on Everest, my apprenticeship was still incomplete. So many teachers, so many ghosts at my back. The Loch of the Green Corrie is sinking deeper in me. We brew up, eat, laze then get back to it. Nothing. Not a nibble, not a rise. MacCaig is chortling in the heaven he doesn't believe in.

Evening settles in. Then dusk. We agree: one last ten minute thrash, then off. We fish with renewed energy, thinking how perfect the narrative would be, to catch something now at the eleventh hour, like France scoring in the dying seconds in the European Cup Final we watched a few days earlier. But nothing. Reel in the last cast. Look around. Break down the rod and leave in the gathering gloom. We're weary, disappointed but not regretful. We've already decided to come back next year, when the wind is westerly and the midgies and fish are biting.

Descent from the Green Corrie

The climb's all right, it's the descent that kills you.
Knees become fists that don't know how to clench
And thighs are strings in parallel.
Gravity's still your enemy: it drills you
With your own backbone – its love is all to wrench
You down on screes or boggy asphodel.

And the elation that for a moment fills you
Beside the misty cairn's that lesser thing,
A memory of it. It's not
The punishing climb, it's the descent that kills you
However sweetly the valley thrushes sing
And shadows darken with the peace they've brought.

Next morning we're finishing breakfast before packing up to leave. We see a policeman coming across the moor and brace ourselves. After all, we have no permits, no permissions. He's come about my car, concerned it's been reported in the same place for three days. He accepts coffee and stays and chats for an hour, more Hamish MacBeth than Hard Cop. He's a keen fisherman. He volunteers that the ban on Sunday fishing is a nonsense, set up by landowners to keep the riff-raff from Glasgow and Fife from coming up for the weekend. Admits sometimes he fishes with a spinner or bait, but if he catches something when the nobs are around, he quickly whips a fly into the fish's mouth. Says if the wind's from the East or North, soon as the air temperature is lower than the water's, fly fishing is useless in these lochs.

He finishes his cigarette and leaves. We christen him the Metaphysical Policeman, come to absolve us of the sins we have failed to commit.

We pack up and hump gear back to the car and drive back to Lochinver which now seems like a metropolis. We're grubby, fish-free but feeling very alive, in touch, refreshed. The homage is done, for this year. As we head South I wonder if in another thirty years some trio will come this way to repeat what we have done, to keep some indefinable faith. In my rear view mirror, the ruined mountains of Assynt recede, and back in South Queensferry, Orkney or Sheffield, live in me yet. As the dead do. As we may in turn.

I don't know where this came from but it's stuck in my head as having something to do with the Loch of the Green Corrie (though it's not called that) trip: *The anticipation of our own death tells us more about anticipation than it does about death.*

Andrew Greig
poems by Norman MacCaig

Cracking Bastions

David Craig

Cracking Bastions
Naming (and Shaming) the Mountains

Napes Needle	Early Days
Pisgah Buttress	
Kern Knotts Crack	
Eagle's Nest Ridge Direct	
Agag's Groove	
Frankland's Green Crack	
Overhanging Bastion	Pre- and Post-War
Devil's Slide	
Savage Slit	
Angels' Highway	
Leopard's Crawl	
Cenotaph Corner	
Moonraker	The Sixties
King Rat	
A Dream of White Horses	
Nagasaki Grooves	
Praying Mantis	
Footless Crow	
Gates of Delirium	Present Day
This Septic Heil	
Rubbelsplitskin	
Cystitis by Proxy	
Screamadelica	
When Dildos Ruled the Earth	

David Craig

Some Scottish Mountain Activities Over the Past 3,000 Million Years

G. F. Dutton

Scottish Mountains: A Metaphorical Imperative

When released from the womb, nest or cage I – like any other animal – continued to explore the outside environment, pressing on where rewarded, sniffing further where not. Being human also, I likewise explored our internal environment, where these incoming data react with themselves and with our processing of them. Such processing when consciously imposed might rank as 'science', otherwise as 'arts'. I find both categories compatible: a continuous spectrum of experience.

I therefore shared life concurrently with as many environments as possible – aesthetic, scientific; urban, rural; aquatic, terrestrial. But here I select mountains, Scottish Mountains; though other parts of the spectrum may intrude.

I explored mountains because they were seen to be *there*; and they promised views of things also *there* but unseen. The exploration was rewarding, physically and metaphysically. Physically, because the body became inured to continuous hard exertion; the brain, to bracing reluctant muscles against the beckonings of gravity; and the whole animal, to enjoy safe travelling over mountains day and night in all weathers with minimum food and shelter. This shunted the rest of life into perspective, revealing unexpected freedom.

The freedom extended into metaphysics. I find metaphor as significant as the stimuli invoking it; and mountains provided panoramas of metaphor. At the very least, you climb out of jungly complexity, the 'blood and mire', to a more rarefied view – glimpsed among swirl from an elevated bog, or cold and clear from some untenable crystalline summit; either way you have achieved a new outlook on your descent. Mountaineering is metaphor acted.

All those explorations of the environment echoed each other, suggesting some underlying unity. As an experimental scientist, I found every turn brought exciting new observations, possibilities to be collected, examined, tested as weight-bearing hypotheses, gingerly – with many rejections – stepped upon; to settle as successive footholds through the flood of the as yet ineluctable. Such discovery exactly paralleled that, say, when climbing roped up rock or ice, or swimming alone along an unknown coast, threshing out a landscape 'garden' at the treeline, or winnowing some new form of verse; experiences all intellectually demanding and imaginatively rich.

However, mountains, especially in Scotland, provide perhaps the most convenient gymnasium in which to practice these antics. Scottish mountains are easily reached – even overnight with torch and moon; they embrace refreshing diversity of form, difficulty and unforgiving climate. So I used them, and they me; workaholic each week, I spent the weekend alone or with chosen companions, sleeping under tent, boulder or open sky, drinking their astringency. I still use them, as home base for *diminuendo* ventures in living.

Companions ... Scottish mountaineers, often as abrasive as that which they climb, range from Bailie Nicol Jarvie through Davie Hume to Braveheart; and to partner this hilariously disputatious clamjamfrie in blizzard and sun, in real, often self-inflicted, peril and to share its canny expertise in happy surviving, wonderfully clears the mind of humbug, spin and non-essentials.

No need to dwell on Difficulty and Danger, those twin fuels of the mountaineering industry. Both are largely relative to the traveller. Braveheart sees neither, where Jarvie fearfully treads: the latter is 'braver', if you like. Danger, since Eve, has always been courted – even Jarvie 'pushes the boat out' his little way. Yet Danger is continually thwarted, too, by ever more ingenious (and expensive) equipment, which allows you still greater exposure, lessened in its turn after a similar ring of the cash register. The whole process entertainingly probes the human dichotomy. I now think it best to travel with minimal technical baggage; then you might recapture some priorities, and the Golden Days.

Our hills possess outstanding 'scientific' interest. You climb through 'Deep Time' – beside you, last week's seedling roots itself into strata weathered before life began – and this yields a thoughtfully holistic satisfaction, less evident in some other great explorations, such as solo swimming through and under wild water. There, the double horizons of sea and shore compete, not collaborate like mountain and glen; and often only the brute compulsion of your lower centres hauls you back from the junkie delight of dissolving into the O-so-caressing Infinite. Bathymetry or marine biology don't get much of a look-in.

Scottish mountains, for me, also peak aesthetically. Other candidate ranges in the world I find limited in comparison – too uniform, too vast for single comprehension, too unstable, too 'messy'. Our hills bulk as if immutable, yet bear the excitement of past adventures burnt into them. Their recent glacial massage ensures a satisfying rhythm, backed by the dominant of the ocean from which they rose.

These surging and syncopated forms, echoing their distances, reproduce for me the great music they have engendered – the luminescent pebble-clean *orain-mòra* and the stark and subtle *piobaireachd*. Nowhere else does the last so resonate: to hear it among the topologically harmonising 'trap' landscapes of Skye is to experience through every sense the unity of what we call Earth, Art and Science, and the life that is permitted to explore them. Pibroch among the Skye mountains is, as MacDiarmid maintained, 'the only fit music for the Last Day'.

Let me conclude with another living function of our hills: as historical grandstand. Almost any summit reveals the passage of buffeted eroded Scotland beneath: from Neolithic hut circles on the lower slopes to the militant industrialism and industrious militarism of the current horizon. At the top of any Scottish hill you stand rooted in the tragi-comic history of this corner of the world, this wave-slapped fragment of rock that – if never enamoured of becoming another Eden – once knew itself as *Tìr nam beann 's nan gleann 's nan gaisgeach*; you become more firmly a member of its thrawn heterogeneous community, besieged, drenched and ransacked by Time, but repeatedly gathering to yet another, evanescent, peak.

as so often in Scotland
the sun travelled
dyke over dyke, burning
dead grass golden and ending,
after a wallow of foothills,
on one brown summit;
that flared its moment, too,
and was gone.

As So Often In Scotland

This Selection is arranged in eight sections touching those physical and social aspects of Scottish mountains possibly less familiar to non-oromaniacs. It stresses mountaineering – once only a sport, now partly game, and increasingly tourism – because mountaineering literature directly reflects social attitudes to our hills and spotlights some of the more amusing human qualities and aberrations. It does *not* represent *current* Scots mountaineering, but selects from the last hundred years which, together with the other 3000 million years of mountain activity, have established the strengths and faults that underlie its present putative attractions. Although the textual continuity of several too space-hungry extracts may suffer from the interposition of ellipses to indicate necessary omissions, the *logical* continuity throughout should be evident. In fact, the running theme of the selection *is* continuity ...

At least 130 mountaineering or hillwalking clubs exist in Scotland, with considerable overlap, for – from isolation and climate – Scottish 'hills' can become mountains and their 'walkers' unwitting mountaineers. The texts emphasise two clubs, the Scottish Mountaineering Club (SMC) and Creagh Dhu Mountaineering Club (CDMC). Both have achieved much, require rigorous election, and once appeared socially elite. They differ piquantly. The SMC displays a hundred years' written records of (usually) douce Edinburgh-Glasgow respectability. The CDMC went on oral record as its hard Clydeside opposite. Most clubs are happy in-betweens, drawn comprehensively from the overpaid, underpaid and unpaid, open to all sexes, some exclusive to organisations, most training their members.

For those wishing to read more of the work here excerpted, the following texts are suggested. For non-, or pre-, mountaineering extracts and references see Ian Mitchell's excellent *Scottish Mountains before the Mountaineers* (Luath Press, 1999), culled from *SMC Journal* histories and some 140 sources including pre-Romantic ones and – at last! – Gaelic hunters and poets. For extensive samples of mountaineering prose and verse see the *SMC Journal* anthology *A Century of Scottish Mountaineering* (ed. Brooker, SMC 1988), and various club journals, especially of the Cairngorm Club and SMC, the latter with 191 numbers since 1890. The CDMC is well covered by Jeff Connor *Creagh Dhu Climber* (Ernest Press, 1999) and savoured by Alastair Borthwick *Always a Little Further* (Mackay, 1939) now published by Baton Wicks; and by Thomson in *May The Fire Be Always Lit* (Ernest Press, 1995) who mentions other penurious clubs, the salt of the sport. Scottish geological history is clearly summarised in Scotland: *The Creation of its Natural Landscape* (McKirdy & Crofts, Scottish Natural Heritage, 1999), and Hutton's work in *James Hutton, The Founder of Modern Geology* (McIntyre & McKirdy, HMSO, 1997), both splendidly illustrated.

Geological History

That part of the Earth's crust we call Scotland has floated like a great ark of rock through all the planet's climatic zones, powered by the magma flow beneath it.

Reflecting this long eventful history, Scotland possesses remarkable geological diversity. Despite equally dramatic later discoveries, the fundamental observations and ideas of James Hutton (the discoverer of 'Deep Time') and his fellow-Scottish successors in the eighteenth and nineteenth centuries founded geology as a science.

Some of the oldest rocks in the world, Lewisian Gneisses, outcrop in north-west Scotland and the Hebrides. Formed over 3,000 million years ago ... their ... ancient landscapes are preserved beneath thick Torridonian sandstones, which were dumped nearly 1,000 million years ago by rivers flowing from vanished eastern mountains.

Until 410 million years ago, Scotland was separated from England by a vast ocean. When these two halves of Britain, then parts of distinct continental landmasses south of the equator, drifted towards each other, the ocean closed and the fragments contributing Scotland slid together along the lines we see today – such as the Great Glen and Highland Boundary faults. England joined Scotland approximately along the route of Hadrian's Wall!

Scottish mountains of Himalayan scale were squeezed up by this impact. These peaks were eroded over millions of years, exposing the granites and gabbros within them. The Cairngorms, Ben Nevis and many other Scottish landmarks are carved from such igneous rocks. Dalradian and Moine sedimentaries, pressed and baked further in this core collision, also remain as higher ground. So our Highland core arose through English opposition!

A calm followed. Scotland, then 10° south of the equator, was mostly mountainous, fringed by isolated freshwater basins. Sand and mud, carried down to these lakes, formed our Old Red Sandstone. As Scotland drifted north to the equator, the lakes became tropical rainforests, source of our coal. Volcanoes and lava flows – as around Edinburgh – were frequent.

During the next 70 million years, great hot deserts – now our New Red Sandstone – covered parts of Scotland, followed by partial submergence under a tropical sea – its shores footprinted by dinosaurs. Another continental rearrangement saw North America and Greenland departing westwards from Scotland on its landmass, to give the – still opening – North Atlantic. Thinned crust at the ocean's margin let volcanoes and lava flows through, from St Kilda to Ailsa Craig, 65–60 million years ago, as now in Iceland; we climb on their ruins today.

Thereafter, major climatic cooling brought several Ice Ages (a much earlier one existed when Scotland lay near the South Pole). The last recent glaciers melted (temporarily?) some 10,000 years ago, and our landform still suffers from their punishment.

Alan McKirdy, 2000

Perhaps ninety-nine hundredths of this earth, so far as we can see, have been formed by collecting loose materials, and depositing them at the bottom of the sea; consolidating [them] and either elevating those consolidated masses, or lowering the level of that sea.

James Hutton, 1788

On us who saw these phenomena for the first time, the impression ... will not easily be forgotten ... We felt ourselves ... carried back to the time when the schistus on which we stood was yet at the bottom of the sea, and when the sandstone before us was only beginning to be deposited, in the shape of sand or mud, from the waters of a superincumbent ocean. An epoch still more remote presented itself, when even the most ancient of these rocks, instead of standing upright in vertical beds, lay in horizontal planes at the bottom of the sea, and was not yet disturbed by that immeasurable force which has burst asunder the solid pavement of the globe. Revolutions still more remote appeared in the distance of this extraordinary perspective. The mind seemed to grow giddy by looking so far into the abyss of time; and while we listened ... to the philosopher [Hutton] who was now unfolding to us ... these wonderful events, we became sensible how much further reason may sometimes go than imagination venture to follow.

John Playfair, 1805

The result, therefore, of our present enquiry, is that we find no vestige of a beginning – no prospect of an end.

James Hutton, 1788

In no respect are the Scottish mountains more interesting than in the wide differences of age which they manifest ... The most ancient of all ... rise to the east of Loch Maree ... One by one they are emerging again to daylight, as their mantle of hardened shingle and sand is being stripped away ... You can climb their sides, one foot on the red conglomerate that marks their former shorelines, and the other on the grey gneiss that rose ... into dry land.

Sir A. Geikie, 1896

To find these hills, look at the contact between the Lewisian gneiss and the Torridonian sandstone, notably north of Loch Maree on Slioch and

Mullach Coire Mhic Fhearchair. Again, from A894 (Inchnadamph to Kylesku) look at this contact rising over 600m on the north face of Quinag. Conveniently, the contact is exposed at the roadside about 2100m beyond Skiag Bridge on A837. One feels the depth of time recorded here, fingering the gneiss that was weathered before the sandstones were deposited nearly 1,000 million years ago. (Please don't deface this wonderful exposure).

Donald B. McIntyre, 2000

Postscript on Erosion. 'Torridonian' is often capped with quartzite, generating 'infamously' unstable screes, subject of the following ironic couplet of praise, 'current in the district' in 1953 but now, in its turn, with its culture, eroded there completely.

'S i mo rùn Beinn Eighe,
Dh'fhalbhadh i leam is dh'fhalbhainn leatha!

My love is Beinn Eighe;
she with me and I with her would go!

SMC Guide, 1953

Scenery

The tender complexion of Geology, so easily defaced by its unpredictably wayward suitors.

Southern Uplands. Nowhere else in Scotland can the exquisite modelling of flowing hill curves be so conspicuously seen. From the skyline on either side, gentle but boldly-drawn curves of moorland sweep down. These architectural forms remain distinct at all seasons ... But their beauty and impressiveness vary from month to month, almost from hour to hour.

Sir A. Geikie, 1865

Another opinion. I found myself gazing, with surprise, almost disappointment [over a] mere succession of grey waving hills ... monotonous in their aspect, and so destitute of trees that one could almost see a stout fly walking along their profile.

Washington Irving, 1820

The Scottish Highlands have no counterpart on this planet ... comparisons fail to survive even brief examination. What is their distinction? ... First, the astonishing variety of scene ... which may owe its skeleton to geological accidents, but shape, flesh and clothing to our maligned Atlantic atmosphere. This humid climate gives the variety and subtlety of colour. [Second] the Atlantic and the lochs, of all mountain settings the most brilliant. The sweep of sea and winding loch ... has its counterpart in every glen where a burn storms ... and on every moor where water lies at peace in brown pools. The wedding of mountain and water, adorned by untold wealth of growing things from Caledonian pines to sphagnum moss, gives a Highland beauty I have never seen equalled in kind or colour ... The outstanding beauty of the Highland scene has been haphazardly expended and no account kept. Are Scots so blind that they cannot prize it for its own sake?

W. H. Murray, 1963

The Cairngorm Club begs respectfully to bring the question of the Glen Feshie road before the ... Minister of Transport ... It adopted [1918] a resolution urging the construction of a road from Deeside to Speyside through Glen Feshie [to] facilitate access to one of the finest mountain regions in the country.[It again, 1924] unanimously resolved to submit the present representation to the Minister of Transport in support of the Glen Feshie road.

Cairngorm Club Journal, 1925

Letter from President, SMC, to Council of the NTS. As the movement initiated by a group of members of the [SMC] to acquire Dalness Forest [Glen Etive and Upper Glen Coe] and hand it over to the National Trust for Scotland, to be held ... so that the public may have unrestricted access at all times, has now materialized ... *The views of the subscribers follow:* (4) That the hills should not be made easier or safer to climb ... (8) That no shelter of any kind be built on the hills.

P. J. H. Unna, 1937

In November 1997 the last defences of Cairngorm fell. Nothing now prevents the Cairngorm Development Company [from proceeding] to rape the mountain with a funicular railway ... The foam had scarcely dried on the mouths of the handful of Scottish climbers who care about mountains when ... the SMC decided at their annual meeting to erect a windmill beside their CIC hut ... in the bosom of Ben Nevis. This structure will stand eight metres high on a concrete plinth ... a whirling shiny phallus to complement the testicular orange gas bottles which currently disfigure the mountain. Besides bringing the SMC into well-deserved disgrace, this grotesque fantasy ... will undermine the efforts to curb the endless march of pylons and masts across our hilltops.

R. N. Campbell, 1999

Habitations

Cave to cave, hut to hut, sheltering refugees from the Early Postglacial climate, from tribes with the wrong smell, from the odour of Authority, from the deserts of joblessness or of bourgeois tedium. Now exposing the Duality: Comfort v. Communion.

In Assynt. A mile up this glen, at ... about 900 feet, are three caves ... which have several times been excavated. Many bones have been found, of Arctic fox, cave bear, northern lynx, reindeer and man.

SMC Guide, 1953

In Arrochar. Today the only entrances ... are two small holes which appear to lead ... to the bowels of the earth. The only other opening is a hole in the roof, blackened by the smoke of fires ... I smelled kippers, and followed my nose ... to a narrow cleft ... I slid downwards and arrived on the floor of the cave ... A big place – with ... jagged walls and a sloping earth floor ... there were three young men squatting round a fire, frying kippers and dangling ... over the flames a large black pudding.

A. Borthwick, 1939

At Craigallion. A gallon-sized tea-can bubbled between the logs. Someone threw ... tea into the can and remarked ... that it had been a Rodine [rat-poison] container. We were not impressed, we used the Rodine half-gallon ourselves ... In time, faces became names ... Starry, Bones, Sparrow, Peaheid, Scrubbernut, where are you now? Simple-lifers. Not for them the Ramblers' Federation and the Youth Hostels ... We quoted Stevenson and Borrow ... Only the aboriginals lived a simpler life than we ... Are huts the beginnings of a movement to make the mountains fit for climbers rather than the climbers fit for mountains? ... The use of a howff is strictly in line with the ascetic nature of mountaineering ... No other approach gives such close communion with the hills.

J. Nimlin, 1948, 1963

Opening of the SMC's hut on Ben Nevis. When the Great War took away so many of our comrades, my wife and I thought to commemorate our son's passing and to benefit the SMC which, to my family, has been a source of joy and love. [On] the opening day ... snow lay around ... The dinner hour, 7pm, approached. A more perfect menu could not be imagined: Kidney Soup – Potato Soup; Tomato & Egg Salad; Sausages Parfaites; Fruit Salad; Tea & Biscuits. Before ... this repast, our padre, Rev. A. E. Robertson, asked a blessing, and prayed that the hut might be a refuge in time of danger ... As tea was being served, the ... door was violently thrown open, and two ... climbers lurched in ... in a state of exhaustion ... Thus early had our hut justified itself.

W. Inglis Clark, 1929

Bill Smith, on Jacksonville, the Creagh Dhu M.C. 'hut' in Glen Coe. An Army tent blew into the river: 'We fished it out and took it back to ... our regular camping ground. We used to leave it at the side of a sheep fank ... we put a canvas cover on the sheep fank and it has gradually built up from there.'

Over the years it sprouted walls and a door and a chimney and has remained inviolate both from intruders and the National Trust on whose land it stands. The reputation of the Creagh Dhu ensured there were never any trespassers ... and the message would be hammered home by a fusillade of rocks and boulders drenching passing visitors as they attempted to cross the Coupall by the stepping stones.

Smith, on an early NTS sortie: 'I was sat inside ... drumming up when I saw this chap and a woman coming across the stepping stones ... He says: "Is there a Mr Jackson here?" and I told him "No, he's away in America, you'll no get hold of him." So then he starts muttering about permission to build the place and I ... suggested ... he see the police. Of course the police told him it was a good thing ... because if there were any rescues they knew where to find climbers who knew the area.'

Jeff Connor, 1999

The Creagh Dhu were skilled and selfless rescuers.

Hunters, Warriors and Wild Men

Hunters and Warriors, celebrated in Gaelic song and story, continually ranged our hills; as did Wild Men, fugitives from law. That Heroic Age there still? No way: 'It is essential at all times to respect the proprietary and sporting rights, especially during the shooting season, and to avoid disturbing game in deer forests or grouse moors. Issued with the authority of: Scottish Mountaineering Club ... Creagh Dhu Mountaineering Club ...' (SMC Northern Highlands Guide, 1964). Read on.

An eighteenth-century poacher, Lonavey, seen shooting deer on Carn Righ, hastily laid his gun – filled with deer-grease – and his dirk in a cave only he knew. He died in prison. No one found it. A hundred years later, the poacher Farquharson, dodging keepers there, hid in a crack. He went in further – was this Lonavey's cave? If so ... then the gun ought to lie [by tradition] in the direction of the dim line of light ... he advanced towards the shelf of rock, and there lay *a gun and dirk!*

W. McCombie Smith, 1904

From John Kay of the Creagh Dhu: Some of the boys would bury their guns in the ground of the various dosses. A friend of mine ... last time he came over from New Zealand ... had been up to the caves on Ben An and found all his guns in the floor of the cave, greased and wrapped in paper, from twenty years before.

Jeff Connor, 1999

From fellow-member Chris Lyon: 'Our team survived because we carried our cargo on our backs, 150lbs per man. Our equipment was mainly ex-army gear and could be jettisoned and re-purchased without any great loss. Mountain fit, few men could outrun the team on the hill. If one keeper was particularly fleet of foot, any member of our team was a match for any one man and as a fighting unit four of us were a match for any ten ... We took to the high places until night fell and by dawn we had force-marched 30 miles ... It was a good life: kill Monday, sell Tuesday, enjoy the city fleshpots and weekend with the boys ... our army mate confessed he had seen more action and more guns fired in anger in two days with us than in his two years' service in World War Two.'

Jeff Connor, 1999

W. H. Murray ... definitely an establishment figure, recalls entering ... Ben Alder bothy at night to find a sing-song ... Opening the door the notes died abruptly and a dozen young scruffs stared at him ... 'Fishing?' [he] inquired discreetly. 'No' said one, and with a roar the whole chorus, whistle and mouth organ, resumed at the note they had halted ... They were the Creagh Dhu and Murray described them as 'like a band of robbers'. In a shed he found a stag hanging from the rafters.

Jeff Connor, 1999

The exuberantly unofficial Creagh Dhu activities recounted above, allegedly occurred before or just after the last war. The Guidebook extract suggests that the CDMC is today as painstakingly conventional as the SMC.

Travel

Wonderful tales remain uncollected, unwritten, unread. Below, after the Age of Giants, the first hints of the Flood.

Naismith and Gilbert Thomson caught the night train from Glasgow, left Dalwhinnie Station at 3.30am, climbed a wintry Ben Alder ridge, crossed to Ben Alder Lodge, forded the Gaoire, crossed the Moor in a blizzard to Gorstan (no railway yet), forded the Orchy and burst into the Easter 1892 Meet at Inveroran on the stroke of 8pm after 45 miles.

A. E. Maylard, 1892

Such epics were common then. We should travel to Kingussie by night-express on Friday ... bicycle thence to Fort William, climb our mountain [Nevis, north face] on arrival, and return by the same route, reaching town on Sunday evening ... *They did reach Edinburgh at 6.15pm after 45 hours continuous travelling, except for an hour's sleep at the Summit Observatory.*

W. Brown, 1895

Foreshadowing that magic carpet of the mid-century Impecunious, the Club Bus. Members should send their name and arrange preliminaries as to tents, etc; or ... Tortoise Sporting Waggon ... There might be that pleasure derivable from meeting with kindred spirits, and the romance inseparable from camping out.

Anon, *SMCJ*, 1890

But: ... a motor car seemed to open up a new era, when we could drive to ... our climb and count the miles between Clachaig and Kingshouse as but dust in the balance [Not always; when the 'beastie' broke down] a sorry nag was procured, harnessed to the car with ropes, and amid the jeers of passersby ... past 11pm ... we slowly paced Princes Street ... Beside such strains as these, the terrors of the Crowberry Ridge and Chasm seemed trifling.

W. Inglis Clark, 1903

The Kingshouse party having departed on their cycles, the motorists followed and overtook them, to be overtaken in their turn on the steepest part of the road – where BR68 refused to mount the rough surface until the baggage had been taken out ... while a heavy shower and jeering cyclists added to the general joy.

G. B. Gibbs, 1906

Impecunious climbers later hitch-hiked. Given two or more hard-bitten and hostile hitch-hikers infesting the same stretch of road, the game becomes more than a gamble on empty seats and sympathetic drivers. It becomes a battle of wits ... for the one rule in competitive hitch-hiking is that the last man gets the first lift ... the man who lags farthest behind is the first to be overtaken by passing traffic and ... has the advantage of ... more energetic souls who walked on ahead. Consequently, fantastic battles have been waged by rival hitch-hikers who have tried to walk fast enough to reach their destination in the event of no lifts being obtainable, and slow enough to remain last all the time.

A. Borthwick, 1939

[Or, before that bus, hired lorries] ... of the covered-waggon type, murderously cold in winter, always overloaded and not entirely legal. Innocent-looking lorries would roll out of Glasgow crammed with suffering climbers. One such [stuck in] the tramlines of a busy street ... after some minutes it began to move in jerks. Someone peered out between the tarpaulins and saw tram-drivers, conductors and policemen bursting their braces to get it clear ... He signalled for silence, but a whisper came 'If the polis ask what's in the lorry, make a noise like sheep'.

J. Nimlin, 1963

[The club buses] ... would race and glower at each other all the way north, fighting for the single chip stop ... [On the way back] ... the songs roared from Kirriemuir to *Gleann a' Chaolais* ... smut and slop from all tongues, great lungfuls that steamed up the air and rivered down the windows, so thick they choked out the diesel and the tyres.

'Anonanon', *SMCJ*, 1960

Early Climbing

What a strange mixture these Victorian climbers were! What kind of men dance reels in the moonlight in Glenfalloch before retiring to soap their stockings and rub muttonfat and whisky into their blisters?

R. N. Campbell, 1999

Their equipment had been delayed. Our climbing gear was made up of a dozen yards of light rope (window sash cord, in fact), calculated ... sufficiently strong for two, an ice axe carried by Naismith, and an alpenstock carried by the writer. The latter had its spike broken off the day before, and rejoiced now in a large nail with the head filed off ... *They nevertheless did good work on the undescribed Glencoe hills.*

Gilbert Thomson, 1890

[With only one poor axe] ... we thought of returning ... but decided it was weak to be done out of our hill, and that it would be more difficult to return than advance ... a slip would have sent us ... by a rapid glissade and ... a terrible fall, over the cliffs below ... The next year I took an axe with me over the Glen Finnan hills, and the shepherds, keepers and others thought my party was surveying for the railway! They were very polite in consequence.

C. Phillip, 1890

At Lochearnhead station our axes caused a police constable to enquire ... if we were prospecting for gold! ... The navvies at the new railway works were much excited, thinking we were brethren on the lookout for a job ... The chief burden of step-cutting fell upon Munro who ... even in the midst of the blizzard ... broke out into snatches of the Club Song.

C. Campbell, 1893

Difficulties of a Laird ... I had a good deal of step-cutting to do, with my axe held close up to the head, so steep was the angle. I was much hampered, too, by having an Inverness cape on.

H. T. Munro, 1891

[The Blackwater Dam navvies] ... were awful thirsty ... They used to climb over the back glen there, down to Kingshouse Inn, and get fou. And then they would try to get back over the glen again, in the dark, and the bog, and the snow. I used to go up with the pony in the spring, when the snow melted. I've brought down as many as twenty. Poor devils. You'd maybe see a boot or an arm sticking out of drift, and then dig ... last year ... I came on a skeleton. Ay. Thirty year it had been there ... There was moss on the bones and a bottle in its hand.

(recounted to) A. Borthwick, 1939

Birth of the Ladies' Scottish Climbing Club. The idea of a Ladies Climbing Club has often been mooted ... The Club has not been idle. A meet was held at Arrochar ... easy and difficult routes were surmounted by the ladies, seven in number; nor were they merely fairweather sportswomen, for ... the whole party returned ... in the highest spirits, but soaked with rain.

Anon, *SMCJ*, 1908

Ladies were grudgingly admitted to the SMC in 1989; pleasingly, men – even gentlemen – are not yet admitted to the LSCC – which has always maintained high standards of climbing.

Forecasting the Vandals (1). Snow at Ryvoan. I deemed it prudent ... not to proceed further, but burst open the door of the bothy. Some of the furniture [and] a quantity of paraffine, had to be sacrificed to make a fire.

A. I. M'Connachie, 1890 (refers to 1870-80)

Forecasting the Vandals (2). Snow on the Campsies. The skis were not much use when ascending, but upon level ground ... better progress was made with them than without them, and a very slight gradient was sufficient to get up tremendous speed during the descent. When ... too steep to risk, the skis were taken off and turned into an improvised toboggan. Skis might often be employed with advantage on winter ascents in Scotland, or rather descents ... In the Alps it is not unlikely that the sport may eventually become popular.

W. V. Naismith, 1892

Later Climbing

The Duality of Risk and Avoidance has now 'progressed' – as Nimlin foresaw – to perforating rock with battery-operated hammer-drills and driving in bolts. Ice-boring vanishes on thaw, but this bores for ever. The boltless contributions, on rock and ice and paper, by such as Marshall and Robin Smith, are creative uses of advanced technique. Those two and their companions from the mid-fifties onwards, taking up what Murray's group pioneered immediately pre- and post-war (and what their predecessors pioneered before them), brought Scottish winter climbing to the forefront of world mountaineering.

Members may be divided into two classes ... those whose ambition is to scale the inaccessible side of peaks ... who look upon a quarry face with fond enthusiasm, as affording chances quite as great, and nearly as glorious, of getting badly hurt, as a genuine mountain does ... I admire these people; I like to dine with them, and hear them talk ... I call them the Ultramontanes ... But let me confess ... that I have permanently enlisted in the Salvation Army ... we are those who like to know that we are safe – absolutely safe. We don't like contusions; we would rather go home to dinner than lie on the ground till people come to set our bones or carry us off on a stretcher; we have no desire to be the conscious element of an avalanche or a land-slip.

H. H. Almond, 1893

Today, Salvationists, as ski-mountaineers, ski the Haute Route Ecossaise *from Mt. Keen to Lochaber and beyond; Ultramontanes unleash Extreme Skiing down ghastly gullies and couloirs. Neither disfigure their mountains.*

A Scottish First Aid: ... we accomplished it by the aid of a 'piton' which we fortunately had with us. This being driven into a crevice in the rock, and the rope passed through its ring ... we reached the bottom of the great cleft.

T. F. .S. Campbell, 1892

Technical Ethics. I t was a cardinal principle that we took the crags as we found them, sculpted by time for recreation and delight. It was permitted to clutch them, rasp them with nails and build small cairns on their ledges, but never to add projections or make holes in them ... Then came the piton. Unlike his predecessors, the new climber did not retreat from the impasse ... and leave the field for the better man. He hammered in a piton and thus implied that if he could not advance without one, neither could his successor.

J. Nimlin, 1958

Technical Practice: Now Dougal is a bit thick and very bold, he never stopped to think, he put bits of left arm and leg in the crack and the rest of him over the right wall and beat the rock ferociously and moved in staccato shuffles out of the sling and up the Corner. I shifted uneasily on my slab which tapered into the overhangs, making eyes at my two little piton belays. As Dougal neared his ledge he was slowing down, but flailing all the time, left fingers clearing out grass in the rock and right leg scything moss on the wall. I pulled down the sleeves of my jersey and took a great grip of the ropes ... Then there came a sort of squawk as Dougal found his ledge was not. He got a hand on it but it all sloped. Rattling sounds came from his throat or nails or something. In his last throes trying to bridge he threw his right foot at a straw away out on the

179

right wall. Then his fingers went to butter. It began under control as the bit of news "I'm off", but it must have caught in the wind, for it grew like a wailing siren to a bloodcurdling scream as a black and bat-like shape came hurtling over the roof with legs splayed like webbed wings and hands hooked like a vampire. I flattened my ears and curled up rigid into a bristling ball, then I was lifted off my slab and rose five feet in the air until we met head to foot and buffered to a stop hanging from the runners in the roof.

Robin Smith, 1960

An Ultramontane, Robin Smith. He was one of the hardest climbers I have known. His strength and perseverance were shattering. On one climb he hung on a problem, spending five or six hours to gain ten feet ... On his winter ascent of Gardyloo he cut for six hours to overcome the near-vertical 150-foot prow ... He delighted in impromptu, unexpected incidents which could impress one's memory indelibly with a sense of satisfying fulfilment or wild belonging to the mountain world ... We are best to remember him by his wild whoops, the tuneless ballads wailing from some fearful dank wall, the hair-raising climbs far into the night and his wanderings about the moonlit snows of the Highland summits.

J.R. Marshall, 1963

The incentive for the whole thing – that 'Unity' again. It is this quality which is the surprising product of the modern age, that the routes penetrate the great 'impossible walls' by tenuous threadlike weaknesses, inducing the greatest concentrations of routefinding technique, with a commensurate heightening of the appreciative senses. Completion of one of these great routes is somewhat akin to the sensation of emerging from the 'engulfment' of a great piece of music or painting.

J. R. Marshall, quoted by W. H. Murray, 1964

Munrosis

Munro (later Sir Hugh) listed, from O.S. maps and exhaustive measurements, all 3000-foot hills in Scotland, and their contentiously-defined Subsidiary Tops, thereby initiating the 'Scottish disease'. Munro-bagging, or -bragging, provides unrivalled knowledge of our mountains, outdoor exercise, indoor arithmetic and a tangible point for a wet day. Hunting out Subsidiary Tops needs luck as well as skill, for heights elevate or erode in learned articles and O.S. computers much as they have done through Geological Time. A dreadful parasitic development lists Completers also; your name is immortalised. The Elect now number 2006, and their hills are showing it. An entire industry tabulating Tops, Subsidiaries and Completers, with perennial Additions, Deletions and Emendations, seems ensured. Such tables should 'receive the study they deserve'. To sample this deadpan grotesquerie consult The Munroist's Companion *edited by R. N. Campbell. It is neatly paralleled by the Ultramontanes' incessant reports of New Climbs in the* SMC *Journal: microscopically described, checked – and contested – for priority and publicity, just like their counterparts in other scientific journals; to the onlooker as intimidating as the Higher Mathematics of Munröology.*

The immense amount of labour undertaken by Mr Munro will be apparent even on the most cursory survey of his 'Tables'. Measured merely by time, the compilation has to my knowledge – for I have been somewhat of a taskmaster in the matter – occupied over three hundred hours during some five months ... There is little doubt that the lists will receive the study they deserve at the hands of all who are interested in the mountains of Scotland.

J. G. Stott, 1891

View of Munro. I saw him as a lone figure in an Inverness cape with a Balmoral on his head, the snow crunching under his boots in that rolling world of mountains … from Angus to Braemar. I see him stopping on top after top, to get out his aneroid and make an entry in a notebook.

T. Weir, 1999

Slioch. The summit is unfortunately furnished with two pimply tops with very little between them (LF01 and LFO9). This … has led to a pleasant game of ping-pong in the Tables, now resolved in favour of LF09. Occasionally and absurdly, both tops have been in the Tables at once.

R. N. Campbell, 1999

Sir Hugh died with three Tops to go … I formed the opinion that something should be done about this regrettable state of affairs … Light-hearted and tasteless discussion … eventually arrived at … constructing an effigy of Munro and transporting the object to the three missing Tops … The effigy … bore a tolerable resemblance to Munro and was sufficiently lifelike – or deathlike – to frighten visitors to my home severely … It could be strapped to a packframe.

Sir Hugh's traverse of the 538 Tops of his 1891 Tables was begun in May 1879. At … his death in 1919, 535 Tops had been visited. Carn an Fhidhleir and Carn Cloich-mhuillin were ascended last year … [He] completed his round of Tops on Wednesday with an ascent of the Inaccessible Pinnacle … this round has therefore occupied 113 years and must be considered as a strong candidate for the Slowest Completion of the Tops.

R. N. Campbell, 1992

Campbell's two wonderful Holmes stories possibly excel those of Sir Arthur. The following is one of the many peaks of The Case of the Great Grey Man: ... Some weeks later a small parcel arrived at Baker Street, bearing a Scottish postmark. Holmes opened it ... and held up two thin octavo volumes bound ... in green calf.

"A note from Munro, Watson", he announced. "Two copies of his list of Scottish mountains ... One for you and one for me. An excellent souvenir of the case, certainly. However, I judge it best to cast mine into the fire." With a deft twirl ... he sent Munro's gift spinning into the flames.

"Holmes! How could you!" I cried ... "The gift was well meant and Munro is surely a friend!"

"Certainly, Watson, but we have so far ascended three mountains on his list. There remain 535. Surely you do not care to spend the rest of your life travelling to Scotland to complete the task."

"Indeed no," I protested, "but I feel no such compulsion."

"Then why did you take the trouble to visit Cairngorm of Derry ... when you thought me asleep? And why do your fingers itch now for a pencil to place four ticks ...? No, my friend, be mindful of the trouble I have with my ... cocaine ..."

I admitted the wisdom ... and regretfully added my gift to the blaze. "Lochaber no more!" said Holmes with a smile ...

R. N. Campbell, 1986

Beta
Glossary
Dan Shipsides

Angel's Wall

Solo.
Low between broken boulders and wall,
L foot jam behind detached flake,
L small fingernail nitch,
nudge up high into 3 finger pocket pull,
R foot wide lever up on L jam,
L hand scoop lip,
push up on feet to thin toothy edge,
hands into good pockets,
swivel L side-on feet high in scoop,
push up to higher-up slanting scoop,
trending Rwards hand over hand last finger joints to under hanging block,
undercling crevice two hands hunch up knees,
feet up smear on crystals and nipples,
R hand big reach low runnel on blind R block push feet,
lever nervy layout L to great hold on top,
wildly break loose with solid dyno up front block,
wobble bloody kneed onto block.
rock up on massive ripples,
to safe.

The Fear

Trad.
Illegal lofty 2nd belay stance,
stand with head in big notch,
tip toe on lip above way way down crashing sea,
hex and thread,
pressure palms on gritty shelves beside the notch,
twist left leg out reach back hook hip-busting shelf,
squeeze down and flip R hand onto flimsy higher plate,
2 hands on plate and swing legs onto big L shelf,
wriggle body onto cramped chosy ledge,
cam,
calm down,
swivel out reach up R hand onto big hold pull up,
hex,
gain L hold clamber up big blind jugs trending L to roof,
cam,
crouch using honeycomb holds under roof L R L R,
shimmy feet L R L R to hanging arete,
safe big horizontal break,
2 cams,
lean out underhang big ears feet in break look around arete,
retreat,
think things through,
reach and pull round onto steep L wall high above the pounding mash
    and sharks,
nuts,
pump up crack and jugs past rusty piton,
wire,
desperate elvis mantle onto lookout top,
smile for the Nikon flashes,
watch for rangers' patrol.

Gecko Roof/Clocks

Bolts.
Back cave least steep wall,
R hand in small pock L foot on bulge pullpush up,
into roof establish 3 fingers R big jug L,
shuffle feet L high crossed through for balance,
clip,
pumpy moves on positive lips,
hang straight arms toe twists in crannies,
clip,
lurch under roof to heel hook scoops,
rest 2 big gripped pockets with opposite pull,
clip,
squeeze fucker pinch on L desperate lunge at forward undercling R then
L,
toe hook keep feet up,
R L pull up lock-off,
clip,
slap R hand big ledge on right beyond lip,
stiffly swing out legs to dangle,
pull up thrutch L hand to notch,
clip,
R foot on ribbed roof edge,
snatch golem with R and lift feet onto lip,
pullstep up and mantle home.

Dan Shipsides

Glossary

Anchor Point where a rope is fixed to the rock. (d) Fixpunkt/Verankerung, (f) Relais/Point d'assurage/Ancrage (de securite), (f-c) Point d'ancrage, (nl) Zekeringspunt, (i) Ancoraggio, (e) Anclaje/Punto de seguro, (s) Ankare/Forankring.

Beta Insider information about a climb. Running or auto beta is someone telling you how to do the moves as you go (as in "can you please shut up with that running beta, I want to find out myself"). (d) Informationen vor dem Start, (f) Description de la voie, (i) Informazioni.

Chickenhead Sometimes phallic shaped, protruding lumps that make excellent hand or footholds on granite, etc. (d) Zacke/Felskopfel, (f-c) Banane, (e) Chile/cuerno.

Dyno/Lunge Dynamic movement towards a distant hold. (d) Dynamo, (f) Jete, (nl) Dynamo, (i) Lancio, (e) Movimiento dinamico, (s) Dynamiskt move.

Elvis, to To have a sewing machine leg. Named after 'Elvis, the King', who suffered from this this problem when singing before a crowd of screaming women. (d) Nahmaschine, (e) motoneta, (pl) telegrafowac.

Flash To lead a climb with no falls or dogging and with no previous attempts on the climb. Two variations exist: the onsight flash (where the climber has never seen the climb before) and the beta flash (where the climber has studied the climb before or has seen someone do the climb). (f) Enchaner en tete.

Grounder A fall where the kinetic energy is not absorbed by the rope and pro but by mother earth itself. Can hurt badly. (d) Bodensturz.

Hangdog, (to dog a move). Climbing, lowering, climbing again till a certain move is made (d) Ausbouldern, (nl) Jo-jo.

Italian hitch Munter hitch knot or HMS knot (f) Noeud a friction de Munter/Noeud de demi-cabestan

Jam, to Wedging body parts in a crack. (d) Klemmen, (f) Faire un verrou/Faire un coincement/Coincer/Verrouiller, (i) Incastrarsi, (e) Encunar, (e-argentina) Empotrar, (s) Jamma, (pl) Klinowac.

Krab (Karabiner) Metal connecting device (aka "biner"). (d) Karabiner, (f) Mousqueton, (nl) Karabiner/mousqueton, (i) Moschettone, (e) Mosqueton/Mosquete, (s) Karbin/Karbinhake, (pl) Karabinek.

Layback/Lieback Somewhat clumsy looking climbing technique where hands and feet work in opposition. (d) Piazen/Dulfer, (f) Dulfer/Lay-back, (i) Dulfer (Opposizione), (e) Dulfer, (s) Layback.

Munge The dirt and vegetation that can sometimes be found in cracks. (f) Herbes.

Needle Rock with a characteristic pointed shape. Also known as pinnacle, aiguille, gendarme, etc. (d) Nadel/Spitze, (f) Aiguille/Gendarme/Pic, (i) Guglia/Pinnacolo, (e) Aguja, (s) Pinnakel.

"Off Belay" Yelled when the climber no longer requires a belay (e.g. because s/he has reached a stance). Once the belayer hears "off belay", s/he removes the rope from the belay device and yells "belay off". In UK, Australia and New Zealand: "Safe". (d) "Stand" ("Aussicher"), (f) "Relais" or "Vache", (nl) "Stand", (i) "Posto"/"Molla", (e) "Libre", (e-argentina) "autoasegurado", (s) "Lagg av"/"Ta hem".

Pumped The feeling of overworked muscles. Most climbers are familiar with the forearm pump: too much finger work causes the forearms to swell and the strength to disappear. With a serious forearm pump, even holding a glass of beer can become a serious challenge. (d) Dicke arme (or any other body part), (f) Avoir les bouteilles/Daube, (nl) Verzuurd, (i) Acciaiato, (s) Pumpad.

Quickdraw, quick Short sling with karabiners on either side. (d) Expressschlinge, (f) Degaine/Couple/Paire, (nl) setje, (i) Rinvio/Preparato/sveltina, (e) cintas express, (s) Expresslinga/Kortslinga, (pl) Expres.

Runout Distance between two elements of pro. A route is 'runout' when the distance between those two elements of pro becomes uncomfortably long. (d) Abstand zwischen 2 Sicherungspunkten, (f) (Une voie est) Engagee, (i) Via protetta lunga, (e) Ruta poco protegida.

Smearing Foot technique where a big part of the climbing shoe is used to generate as much friction as possible. The opposite of edging. (d) Auf reibung stehen, (f) Adherence de pieds, (i) Aderenza, (e) Friccion, (s) Smeara.

Trad Traditional climbing, characterized by the placing of protection (cams, nuts, etc.) in cracks and pockets. Trad also includes multi-pitch routes often with long runouts. (d) Traditionelles, Alpines Klettern, (f) Classique, (nl) Alpijns klimmen, (i) Tradizionale, (e) Escalada tradicio-nal/clasica.

Undercling A hold that would be a perfect bucket if gravity were upside down. As it is, underclings are usually awkward holds that require lieback type moves. (d) Untergriff, (f) Inversee/Aile de poulet, (nl) Ondergreep, (i) Presa rovescia, (e) Undercling, (e-argentina) Toma invertida, (pl) podchwyt.

Verglas Thin water ice on rock. (f) Verglas.

Woodie A homemade climbing wall. (f) Pan.

Yabo As in 'yabo start'. A 'sit start'. Named after John Yablonski a stud southern California climber nicknamed Yabo.

Zipper A fall where the protection pulls out one after the other as the leader succumbs to gravity. Often ends with a grounder (or a cardiac arrest). (d) Reissverschlusssturz.

Compiled by Dan Shipsides
from 'The Climbing Dictionary' by Carl Ockier

Author Notes

Author Notes

Neal Beggs

Neal Beggs was born in 1959 and lives and works in Glasgow. He currently has a Scottish Year of the Artist residency with the Mountaineering Council of Scotland. The *Corridor*, a book based on work at the CCA is due out this year.

David Craig

David Craig was born in Aberdeen in 1932 and has a daughter and three sons. He is married to Anne Spillard and lives in Cumbria within sight of the English Highlands. His recent books are: *Native Stones* (1987), *On the Crofters' Trail* (1990), *The Grasshopper's Burden* (1992), *Landmarks* (1995), and *Arch* with Andy Goldsworthy (1998). He is currently working on *Glens of Silence: Landscapes of the Clearances* with the photographer David Paterson.

G. F. Dutton

Geoffrey Dutton is an Hon. Member of the SMC and former editor of the *SMC Journal*. His humorous stories on Scottish mountaineering are are now in third edition as *The Complete Doctor Stories* (Baton Wicks, 1999). He has won awards for his poetry collections *Camp One,* (MacDonald, 1978), *Squaring the Waves* and *The Concrete Garden* (Bloodaxe, 1986 &1991). *The Bare Abundance,* selected poems, is due from Bloodaxe, 2001.

Gerrie Fellows

Gerrie Fellows' most recent collection of poetry is the *The Powerlines*, (Polygon, 2000) She lives in Glasgow with her husband Tom Prentice (with whom she has shared various mountaineering adventures) and their daughter.

Andrew Greig

Andrew Greig is the author of six acclaimed books of poetry and two mountaineering books, *Summit Fever* and *Kingdoms of Experience* (Canongate, 1997 &1999). His novels *Electric Brae* and *The Return of John Macnab* were shortlisted for major prizes. His most recent novels, *When They Lay Bare* and *That Summer*, are published by Faber.

Stewart McGavin

Stewart McGavin is a retired academic scientist who took up writing verse because of an interest in Scots.

Tom Prentice

Tom Prentice is a freelance editor and journalist, Publications Manager for the Scottish Mountaineering Club and one-time editor of *Climber* magazine. He lives in Glasgow with his wife Gerrie Fellows and their daughter.

Dan Shipsides

Dan Shipsides is an artist and climber based in Belfast. He won the Nissan Public Art project 2000 in Dublin and the Perspective 98 Award. His work engages a point where climbing and art meet, developing a dynamic approach to representing landscape in art. He is currently engaged in an AHRB fellowship at the University of Ulster.

Kenneth White

Kenneth White was born in Glasgow and raised on the West Coast of Scotland. He settled in France in 1967 and now lives on the north coast of Brittany. Polygon have recently published *On Scottish Ground* (essays) and *House of Tides*, a book centred on Brittany. In 1989 White founded the International Institute of Geopoetics, which now has centres in various countries.

Colin Will

Colin Will was born in Edinburgh and now lives in Dunbar. He is a scientific librarian by profession, currently in senior management at the Royal Botanic Garden in Edinburgh; a naturalist, hill-walker and writer by inclination. Two of his poetry collections have been published *Thirteen Ways of Looking at the Highlands and More* (Diehard, 1996) and *Seven Senses* (Diehard, 2000).

Photographer Notes

David Paterson

David Paterson was born in 1945. He turned to photography in 1971 after a brief career in the oil industry and worked for twenty-five years as a commercial photographer. Since the late 1980s he has published a number of books on landscape and related themes. He has a;so maintained a long-running collaboaration with the poet and artist Ian Hamilton Finlay.

List of Photographs

Index of Authors

Acknowledgements

Thanks are due to the following copyright holders for permission to reproduce the extracts and poems in this collection. While every effort has been made to trace and credit copyright holders, the Publishers will be glad to rectify any oversights in any future editions.

ALASTAIR BORTHWICK: extracts from *Always a Little Further* (© Diadem/Baton Wicks). JEFF CONNOR: extracts from *Creagh Du Climber* (© Ernest Press, 1999).JIM CRUMLEY: 'The Key to a Fragile Silence'. SETON GORDON: 'Beside Loch Eanaich', from *The Cairngorm Hills of Scotland*, (© Cassell, 1925). JORIE GRAHAM: 'Vertigo' from *The Dream of the Unified Field* (© Carcanet Press Ltd, 1996). PETER HANDKE: extract from *Mont Saint-Victoire*, trans. Ralph Mannheim (© Methuen, 1985). PRIMO LEVI: extract from *The Periodic Table*, (Michael Joseph, 1985), trans. Raymond Rosenthal (© Shocken Books Inc., 1984). NORMAN MACCAIG: 'So Many Summers', 'Rich Day', 'Descent from the Green Corrie'. from *Collected Poems* (© Hogarth Press). ANTOINE DE SAINT-EXUPERY: extract from *Wind, Sand and Stars*, (Penguin Classics, 2000), translated by William Rees (© William Rees, 2000). NAN SHEPHERD: 'Living Mountain' from *The Living Mountain*, (Aberdeen University Press, 1977). UILLEAM RYNUIE/WILLIAM SMITH: Translated from the Gaelic by Adam Watson (adapted by David Craig). GARY SNYDER: 'Cold Mountain', (©Fulcrum Press, 1966). WILLIAM STAFFORD: 'Report to Someone' is reprinted with the permission of Confluence Press from *Even in Quiet Places* (© the estate of William Stafford, 1996). I. D. S. THOMSON: extracts from *May the Fire Be Always Lit*, (© Ernest Press, 1995). KENNETH WHITE: 'Reading Han Shan in the Pyrenees', from *The Bird Path* (© Mainstream, 1989) EDWARD WHYMPER: 'Scrambles Amongst The Alps In The Years 1860-69' (© John Murray Publishers Ltd, 1971).

Thanks to SMC Publications for permission to use various extracts from *The Munroist's Companion* (1999), *Northern Highlands Guide* (1953) and *The Cairngorms* (1975); to the editors of the *SMC Journal* for the many excerpts therefrom; to *High* magazine; and to Yuuko Yamaguchi from whose website the climbing Glossary is taken: http://kfn.ksp.or.jp/~yuuko/climbing.

Spring 2001

08   DISTANCE & PROXIMITY
The first collection of Scottish poet Thomas A. Clark's prose
poems, *Distance & Proximity* includes the ever-popular *In Praise
of Walking*, as well as a number of previously unpublished works,
accompanied by the suggestive textures of Olwen Shone's
photographs.
ISBN 0 7486 6288 X paperback, 128pp, £7.99

09   THE WAY TO COLD MOUNTAIN
A Scottish mountains anthology weaving together poetry, nature
writing and mountaineering adventures, edited by Alec Finlay,
with photographs by David Paterson.
ISBN 0 7486 6289 8 paperback, 208pp, £7.99

10   THE ORDER OF THINGS
An anthology of sound, pattern and concrete poems that explore
the grain of language and imitate the forms of nature. Edited by
Ken Cockburn with Alec Finlay; with an accompanying CD.
ISBN 0 7486 6290 1 paperback, 208pp, £7.99 (including VAT)

Autumn 2001

11   MACKEREL & CREAMOLA
      A collection of Ian Stephen's linked short stories with recipe-
      poems, illustrated with children's drawings. *Mackerel &Creamola*
      draws on Stephen's deep knowledge of the Hebrides, sea lore,
      and his experiences as a sailor. Foreword by Gerry Cambridge
      with an accompanying CD.
      ISBN 0 7486 6302 9 paperback, 208pp, £7.99 (including VAT)

12   THE LIBRARIES OF THOUGHT & IMAGINATION
      An anthology of 'Bookshelves' selected by artists and writers,
      and an illustrated survey of artist projects celebrating books and
      libraries. Edited by Alec Finlay, with an an Afterword edited by
      Olaf Nicolai featuring an anthology of imagined books.
      ISBN 0 7486 6300 2 paperback, 208pp, £7.99

13   UNRAVELLING THE RIPPLE
      Book Artist Helen Douglas' beautiful and striking portrait of
      the tideline on a Hebridean island. Published in full colour,
      Unravelling the Ripple unfolds as a single image that flows
      through the textures and rhythms of sand, sea-wrack, rock and
      wave, to reveal dynamic sensual and imaginative depths.
      ISBN 0 7486 6303 7 paperback, 208pp, £7.99

Spring 2002

14   JUSTIFIED SINNERS
      An archaeology of Scottish counter-culture (1960–2000), from
      Sigma and Conceptual Art to the Beltane Fire Festival and
      the K Foundation. Edited by Ross Birrell and Alec Finlay,
      illustrated throughout.
      ISBN 0 7486 6308 8 paperback, 208pp, £7.99

15   FOOTBALL HAIKU
      An anthology of 'Football Haiku' published to coincide with the
      2002 World Cup in Japan and South Korea. Edited by Alec Finlay,
      with photographs by Guy Moreton and an audio CD.
      ISBN 0 7486 6309 6 paperback, 208pp, £7.99 (including VAT)

Available through all good bookshops.

Book trade orders to:
Scottish Book Source, 137 Dundee Street, Edinburgh EH11 1BG.

Copies are also available from:
Morning Star Publications, Canongate Venture (5), New Street,
Edinburgh EH8 8BH.

Website: www.pbks.co.uk

Endpiece: The Needle, The Quirang, Skye